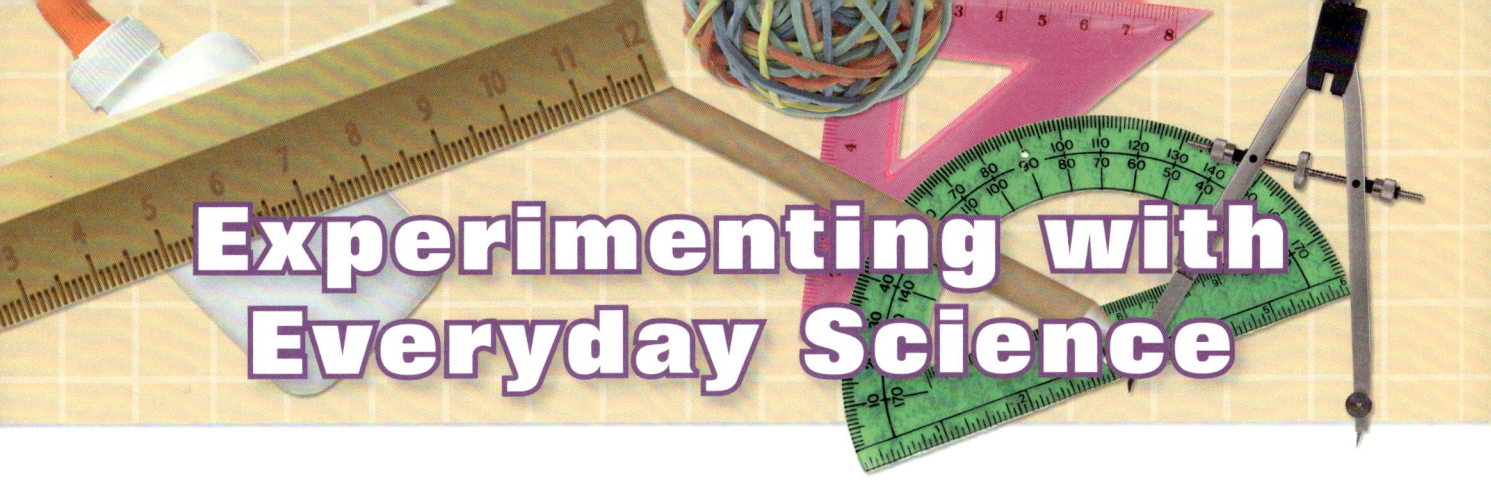

Experimenting with Everyday Science

Music

Experimenting with Everyday Science

Art and Architecture

Food

Man-made Materials

Music

Sports

Tools and Machines

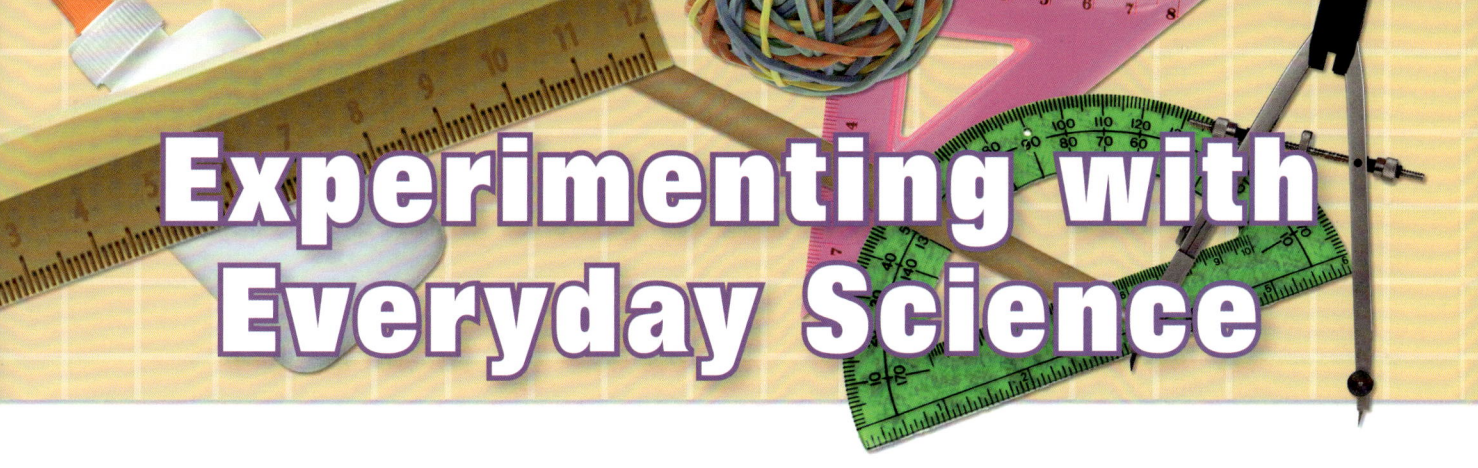

Experimenting with Everyday Science

Music

Stephen M. Tomecek

To Jeff and Andy, my first bandmates, and to Tony Soma, a great music teacher who inspired me to keep learning my craft. You guys rock!

Experimenting with Everyday Science: Music
Copyright © 2010 by Infobase Publishing

All rights reserved. No part of this book may be reproduced or utilized in any form or by any means, electronic or mechanical, including photocopying, recording, or by any information storage or retrieval systems, without permission in writing from the publisher. For information, contact:

Chelsea House
An imprint of Infobase Publishing
132 West 31st Street
New York NY 10001

Library of Congress Cataloging-in-Publication Data
Tomecek, Steve.
 Music / by Stephen M. Tomecek.
    p. cm. — (Experimenting with everyday science)
 Includes bibliographical references and index.
 ISBN 978-1-60413-169-7 (hardcover)
 1. Music—Acoustics and physics—Juvenile literature. 2. Musical instruments—Juvenile literature. I. Title. II. Series.

 ML3805.T66 2009
   781.2'3—dc22   2009022333

Chelsea House books are available at special discounts when purchased in bulk quantities for businesses, associations, institutions, or sales promotions. Please call our Special Sales Department in New York at (212) 967-8800 or (800) 322-8755.

You can find Chelsea House on the World Wide Web at http://www.chelseahouse.com

Text design by Annie O'Donnell
Cover design by Alicia Post
Composition by Mary Susan Ryan-Flynn
Cover printed by Bang Printing, Brainerd, MN
Book printed and bound by Bang Printing, Brainerd, MN
Date printed: April, 2010
Printed in the United States of America

10 9 8 7 6 5 4 3 2 1

This book is printed on acid-free paper.

All links and Web addresses were checked and verified to be correct at the time of publication. Because of the dynamic nature of the Web, some addresses and links may have changed since publication and may no longer be valid.

Contents

Introduction — 7
Safety Precautions: Review Before Starting Any Experiment — 8

1 The Science of Sound — 11
Experiment 1: Selected Sound Makers — 13
Experiment 2: How Vibration Speed and Size Affect Waves — 19
Experiment 3: Making Longitudinal Waves — 24
Experiment 4: Reflecting Sound Waves — 29
Experiment 5: Controlling Instrument Volume — 34
Experiment 6: How Speed of Vibrations Affects Pitch of Sound — 39

2 Early Music Makers — 44
Experiment 7: Controlling the Pitch of Sound with Your Mouth — 45
Experiment 8: Controlling Vocal Cords — 49
Experiment 9: Musical Wood Blocks — 54
Experiment 10: Effect of Tube Length on Sound Pitch — 60
Experiment 11: Song Rhythm vs. Note Timing — 65

3 Instruments with Strings — 69
Experiment 12: Creating Tension on a Vibrating String — 71
Experiment 13: Octaves and Intervals — 75
Experiment 14: Sounds from Vibrating Rubber Bands — 80
Experiment 15: Resonance and Musical Instruments — 84
Experiment 16: Amplifying Sound with Resonators — 89

4 The Wind Instruments — 94
Experiment 17: Controlling the Pitch of Recorders and Song Flutes — 96
Experiment 18: Creating Sounds with a Trombone — 101
Experiment 19: Making a Didgeridoo to Test Resonance — 106
Experiment 20: How a Wind Instrument's Shape Affects its Sound — 110
Experiment 21: Vibrations Through Various Materials — 115

5 Percussion Instruments — 120

Experiment 22: Creating an Idiophone — 122
Experiment 23: Playing Resonant Water Glasses — 126
Experiment 24: Testing Sounds of Metal Bracket Chimes — 130
Experiment 25: Controlling Drum Head Sound — 134

6 Modern Modes of Music — 139

Glossary — 153
Bibliography — 155
Further Resources — 156
Picture Credits — 158
Index — 160
About the Author — 165

Introduction

When you hear the word *science*, what's the first thing that comes to mind? If you are like most people, it's probably an image of a laboratory filled with tons of glassware and lots of sophisticated equipment. The person doing the science is almost always wearing a white lab coat and probably is looking rather serious while engaged in some type of experiment. While there are many places where this traditional view of a scientist still holds true, labs aren't the only place where science is at work. Science can also be found at a construction site, on a basketball court, and at a concert by your favorite band. The truth of the matter is that science is happening all around us. It's at work in the kitchen when we cook a meal, and we can even use it when we paint a picture. Architects use science when they design a building, and science also explains why your favorite baseball player can hit a home run.

In **Experimenting with Everyday Science**, we are going to examine some of the science that we use in our day-to-day lives. Instead of just talking about the science, these books are designed to put the science right in your hands. Each book contains about 25 experiments centering on one specific theme. Most of the materials used in the experiments are things that you can commonly find around your house or school. Once you are finished experimenting, it is our hope that you will have a better understanding of how the world around you works. While reading these books may not make you a world-class athlete or the next top chef, we hope that they inspire you to discover more about the science behind everyday things and encourage you to make the world a better place!

Safety Precautions

REVIEW BEFORE STARTING ANY EXPERIMENT

Each experiment includes special safety precautions that are relevant to that particular project. These do not include all the basic safety precautions that are necessary whenever you are working on a scientific experiment. For this reason, it is necessary that you read and remain mindful of the General Safety Precautions that follow.

Experimental science can be dangerous, and good laboratory procedure always includes carefully following basic safety rules. Things can happen very quickly while you are performing an experiment. Materials can spill, break, or even catch fire. There will be no time after the fact to protect yourself. Always prepare for unexpected dangers by following the basic safety guidelines during the entire experiment, whether or not something seems dangerous to you at a given moment.

We have been quite sparing in prescribing safety precautions for the individual experiments. For one reason, we want you to take very seriously every safety precaution that is printed in this book. If you see it written here, you can be sure that it is here because it is absolutely critical.

Read the safety precautions here and at the beginning of each experiment before performing each activity. It is difficult to remember a long set of general rules. By rereading these general precautions every time you set up an experiment, you will be reminding yourself that lab safety is critically important. In addition, use your good judgment and pay close attention when performing potentially dangerous procedures. Just because the text does not say "be careful with hot liquids" or "don't cut yourself with a knife" does not mean that you can be careless when boiling water or punching holes in plastic bottles. Notes in the text are special precautions to which you must pay special attention.

GENERAL SAFETY PRECAUTIONS

Accidents caused by carelessness, haste, insufficient knowledge, or taking an unnecessary risk can be avoided by practicing safety procedures and being alert while conducting experiments. Be sure to check the individual experiments in this book for additional safety regulations and adult supervision requirements. If you will be working in a lab, do not work alone. When you are working off site, keep in groups with a minimum of three students per group, and follow school rules and state legal requirements for the number of supervisors required. Ask an adult supervisor with basic training in first aid to carry a small first-aid kit. Make sure everyone knows where this person will be during the experiment.

PREPARING
- Clear all surfaces before beginning experiments.
- Read the instructions before you start.
- Know the hazards of the experiments and anticipate dangers.

Safety Precautions

PROTECTING YOURSELF
- Follow the directions step-by-step.
- Do only one experiment at a time.
- Locate exits, fire blanket and extinguisher, master gas and electricity shut-offs, eyewash, and first-aid kit.
- Make sure there is adequate ventilation.
- Do not horseplay.
- Keep floor and workspace neat, clean, and dry.
- Clean up spills immediately.
- If glassware breaks, do not clean it up; ask for teacher assistance.
- Tie back long hair.
- Never eat, drink, or smoke in the laboratory or workspace.
- Do not eat or drink any substances tested unless expressly permitted to do so by a knowledgeable adult.

USING EQUIPMENT WITH CARE
- Set up apparatus far from the edge of the desk.
- Use knives or other sharp-pointed instruments with care.
- Pull plugs, not cords, when removing electrical plugs.
- Clean glassware before and after use.
- Check glassware for scratches, cracks, and sharp edges.
- Clean up broken glassware immediately.
- Do not use reflected sunlight to illuminate your microscope.
- Do not touch metal conductors.
- Use alcohol-filled thermometers, not mercury-filled thermometers.

USING CHEMICALS
- Never taste or inhale chemicals.
- Label all bottles and apparatus containing chemicals.
- Read labels carefully.
- Avoid chemical contact with skin and eyes (wear safety glasses, lab apron, and gloves).
- Do not touch chemical solutions.
- Wash hands before and after using solutions.
- Wipe up spills thoroughly.

HEATING SUBSTANCES
- Wear safety glasses, apron, and gloves when boiling water.
- Keep your face away from test tubes and beakers.
- Use test tubes, beakers, and other glassware made of Pyrex glass.
- Never leave apparatus unattended.
- Use safety tongs and heat-resistant gloves.

- If your laboratory does not have heat-proof workbenches, put your Bunsen burner on a heat-proof mat before lighting it.
- Take care when lighting your Bunsen burner; light it with the airhole closed, and use a Bunsen burner lighter in preference to wooden matches.
- Turn off hot plates, Bunsen burners, and gas when you are done.
- Keep flammable substances away from flames and other sources of heat.
- Have a fire extinguisher on hand.

FINISHING UP

- Thoroughly clean your work area and any glassware used.
- Wash your hands.
- Be careful not to return chemicals or contaminated reagents to the wrong containers.
- Do not dispose of materials in the sink unless instructed to do so.
- Clean up all residues and put them in proper containers for disposal.
- Dispose of all chemicals according to all local, state, and federal laws.

BE SAFETY CONSCIOUS AT ALL TIMES!

The Science of Sound

Maybe you play a musical instrument. Maybe you just like to sing or whistle. Even if you don't have a special musical talent, you can enjoy listening to music. Whether it's rock, hip-hop, classical, or jazz, music is an art form that people have been enjoying for thousands of years.

Most people know what music is when they hear it. Like other forms of art, however, it is difficult to come up with a strict definition of the term. That's because music comes in many forms. The word itself is based on the Greek word *mousike*, which comes from the word *mousa*, meaning "muse." In ancient Greece, the Muses were beings who were thought to control creativity in the arts.

All music involves creating and manipulating sound. Most music has some type of melody or pattern to the sounds that is often repeated to make a song. Even if a song has no clear melody, it usually has some type of beat or rhythm.

Over the course of thousands of years, people have experimented with different styles of music and have discovered many ways of making it. The truth is that being a musician is quite similar to being a scientist. Musicians are always testing new ideas and new materials with which to produce their songs. Being a musician means you have to listen carefully. Listening is a form of observation, and observation is a key step in the scientific method. We are going to look at some of the ways that science influences music. By understanding some of the science behind music, you may gain a better appreciation of how both musicians and the instruments they play create the music you hear.

Because all music involves the manipulation of sound, we'll begin by looking at some of the science that makes sound possible.

SOUND IS ENERGY

Sound is all around us. From the sweet songs of birds in the trees to the roar of a jet engine, we are continuously exposed to sounds. Sound is a form of mechanical energy. Energy is what makes things move. In order for an object to produce a sound, it must somehow start moving.

When something moves back and forth, it **vibrates**. Because different materials vibrate in different ways, they tend to produce different sounds. In **Experiment 1:** *Selected Sound Makers*, you will test to see how the properties of different materials affect how well they vibrate and how well they make sound.

EXPERIMENT 1

Selected Sound Makers

Topic

What properties control the sound a material makes?

Introduction

There is an age-old question: "If a tree falls in a forest, but nobody hears it, does it still make a sound?" From a scientific standpoint, the answer is clearly "yes." That's because as a tree falls, it moves, and any moving object will cause the air around it to vibrate.

The sound produced by a vibrating object is controlled by the physical properties of the object. Size, shape, hardness, density, and flexibility of the material are just a few of the properties that designers must be aware of when they are creating musical instruments. In this activity, you will test to see how the physical properties of different materials help to control the sounds that they produce.

Time Required

45 minutes

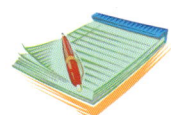

Materials

- large wooden spoon
- metal mixing bowl
- large empty drinking glass
- small block of wood
- pillow
- roll of toilet paper

14 MUSIC

> **Safety Note** No special safety precautions are needed for this activity. Please review and follow the safety guidelines before proceeding.

Procedure

1. Place the items to be tested in front of you on a table or some other sturdy surface. Pick up each object and examine it closely. Describe how each object looks and feels. Record your descriptions on the data table.

2. Pick up the wooden spoon and use it to gently tap the rim of the mixing bowl. Observe what happens to the bowl when you strike it, and describe the sound that it makes. Record your observations on the data table.

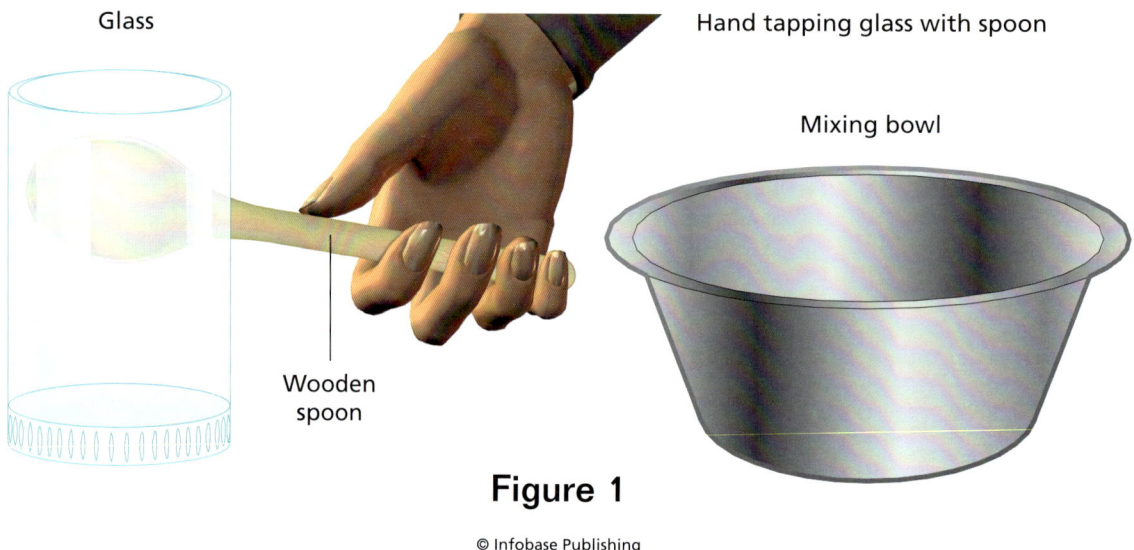

Figure 1

© Infobase Publishing

3. Repeat Step 2 using the drinking glass. Remember to tap the glass *gently* with the spoon so you don't break it.

4. Repeat Step 2 with the remaining items. In each test, try to use the same amount of force when striking the object with the spoon. Based on your tests and observations, think about which physical properties have the greatest affect on the type of sound that an object produces.

Data Table 1		
Object	Description	Type of Sound Produced
mixing bowl		
drinking glass		
block of wood		
pillow		
toilet paper		

Analysis

1. Which object vibrated for the longest amount of time after being struck?
2. What was the effect of hitting the pillow with the spoon? Why?
3. Based on the results of the experiment, which physical property appears to be most important when it comes to an object's ability to vibrate?

What's Going On?

Many physical properties affect the sound that an object will produce. In order for an object to make a sound, it must be able to vibrate freely when mechanical energy is put into it. Some objects will continue vibrating even after the source of the energy has been removed. In this experiment, the vibrations were caused by the wooden spoon striking the object. The mixing bowl and water glass both produced relatively loud sounds, and the vibrations continued well after they were hit with the spoon. Both of these objects are made of hard, dense materials with thin surfaces. When they were struck with the spoon, the surfaces continued vibrating, just as a bell continues to ring after it has been struck.

The roll of toilet paper and the pillow made soft sounds, and the vibrations stopped quickly. Soft materials tend to absorb mechanical energy. As a result, they do not vibrate well and have little ability to make a sound. This is why materials like foam rubber and fabric are often used to help soundproof a room. The wood block made a relatively loud sound, but the vibrations also stopped quickly. Wood is a hard, relatively dense material. But the mass of the block absorbed the mechanical energy, so the vibrations stopped quickly.

Our Findings

Analysis

1. Depending on their sizes, either the mixing bowl or drinking glass should have vibrated the longest and produced the loudest sound.
2. Hitting the pillow with the spoon caused little sound and few vibrations because the pillow was soft and absorbed the impact of the spoon.
3. Hard, dense materials vibrate much better than soft materials do.

ENERGY AND WAVE MOTION

In order to make a sound, you need to get something vibrating. But how does sound travel from the vibrating object to your ear? Sound travels from one place to another in **waves**. Wave motion is an efficient way to transfer energy. Light, heat, radio transmissions, and television transmissions all are carried by waves.

When most people hear the word *wave*, they think of waves of water. Water waves provide a good example of how other waves move, because all waves follow the same basic principles.

Sound travels in waves in the same way waves travel through water: They travel through a substance by creating a disturbance or vibration. A cannonball dive into a pool causes water to push up against the water next to it, leading to a chain reaction and causing waves.

The most important thing to understand about wave motion is that a wave does not actually push a substance (such as water or air) from one place to another. Instead, the wave travels through the substance by creating a disturbance or vibration.

If someone does a cannonball dive into a pool, his or her body touching the water creates a disturbance. A wave will move across the surface of the water from the place where the body hit. It may look as if the water is being pushed out in all directions, but the distance that each water molecule moves is quite small. The disturbance causes the water to push against the water next to it, which sets up a chain reaction of movement. The wave moves quickly across the pool and may even move up over the side, but as soon as the energy is removed, most of the water molecules return to their original positions.

Another example of this phenomenon is when people do a "wave cheer" in a stadium or arena. In this case, people move up and down in a pattern. The "wave" moves through the entire crowd, but each person moves only a small distance. People aren't running around the stadium. In **Experiment 2: How Vibration Speed and Size Affect Waves**, you will test to see how the speed and size of vibrations control the way the waves move.

EXPERIMENT 2
How Vibration Speed and Size Affect Waves

Topic

How do the speed and size of vibrations affect the waves that they produce?

Introduction

Most forms of energy—including sound, light, and heat—travel in waves. Though waves come in several forms, all waves have the same basic parts. Figure 1 shows a drawing of a simple wave. This is the same type of wave that you would find moving along the surface of the ocean.

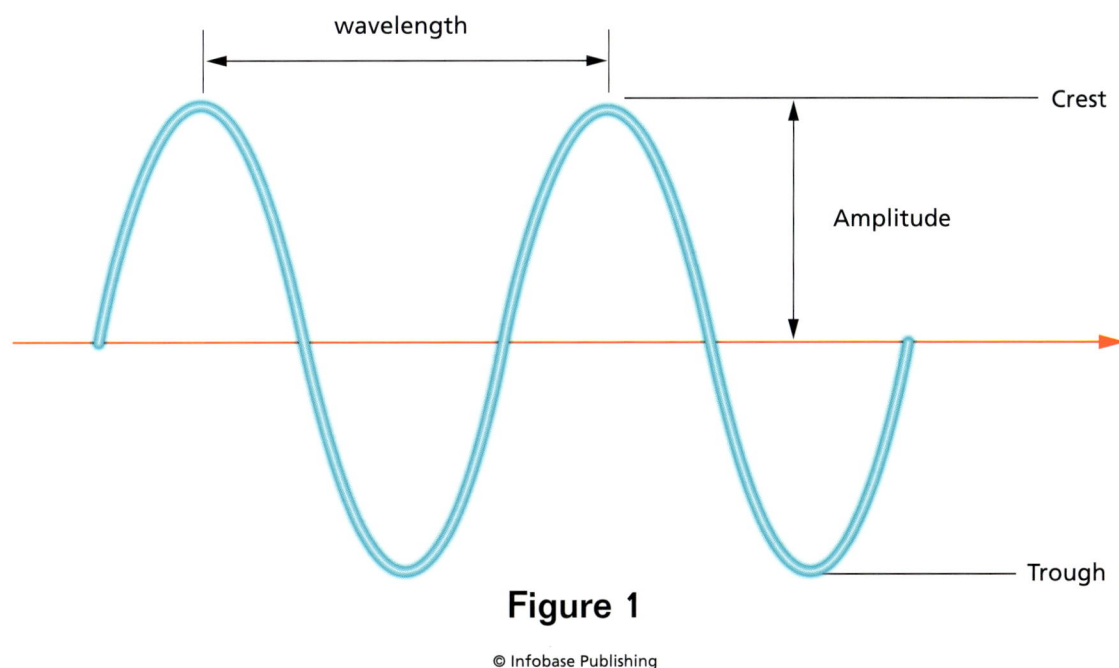

Figure 1

© Infobase Publishing

The highest point of the wave is called the **crest**. The lowest point of the wave is called the **trough**. One **wavelength** is the distance between the same two points on two adjoining waves. A wavelength can be measured from wave crest to wave crest, from trough to trough, or from the midpoints of two adjoining waves. The **amplitude** of a wave is the distance between the midpoint of a wave and the wave crest. In other words, the amplitude is equal to half of the total wave height.

Waves can be thought of as pulses of energy. The number of waves that pass a given point each second is called the **frequency**. Wave frequency is measured in units called **hertz (Hz)**. The unit is named after the German scientist Heinrich Hertz. In the late 1800s, he was the first to demonstrate radio waves. When one wave passes a point in one second, it has a frequency of 1 Hz. Depending on the type of wave, frequencies can range from less than one to billions of Hz. In this activity, you will test to see how changing the energy of a vibrating object controls the amplitude, wavelength, and frequency of a wave.

Time Required

45 minutes

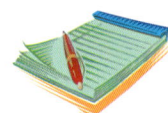

Materials

- piece of thin rope about 10 ft (3 m) long
- timing device to measure seconds
- door knob or some other stationary object to tie the rope to

Safety Note No special safety precautions are needed for this activity. Please review and follow the safety guidelines before proceeding.

Procedure

1. Tie one end of the rope to a door knob or some other large object that won't move easily. Hold the other end of the rope tightly in one hand and stand about 8 ft (2.5 m) from the tied-off end. The rope should be loose, but it should not be touching the floor.

2. Give the end of the rope a single small snap by moving it up and down quickly about 1 ft (30 cm) and observe the pattern in the rope. Repeat the procedure, but this time snap more of the rope so it moves up and down about 2 ft (60 cm). Observe the pattern in the rope.

3. Allow the rope to stop moving. Using the timer as a guide, give the rope a small snap once per second for five seconds. Watch the pattern that develops in the rope and record your observations on the data chart.

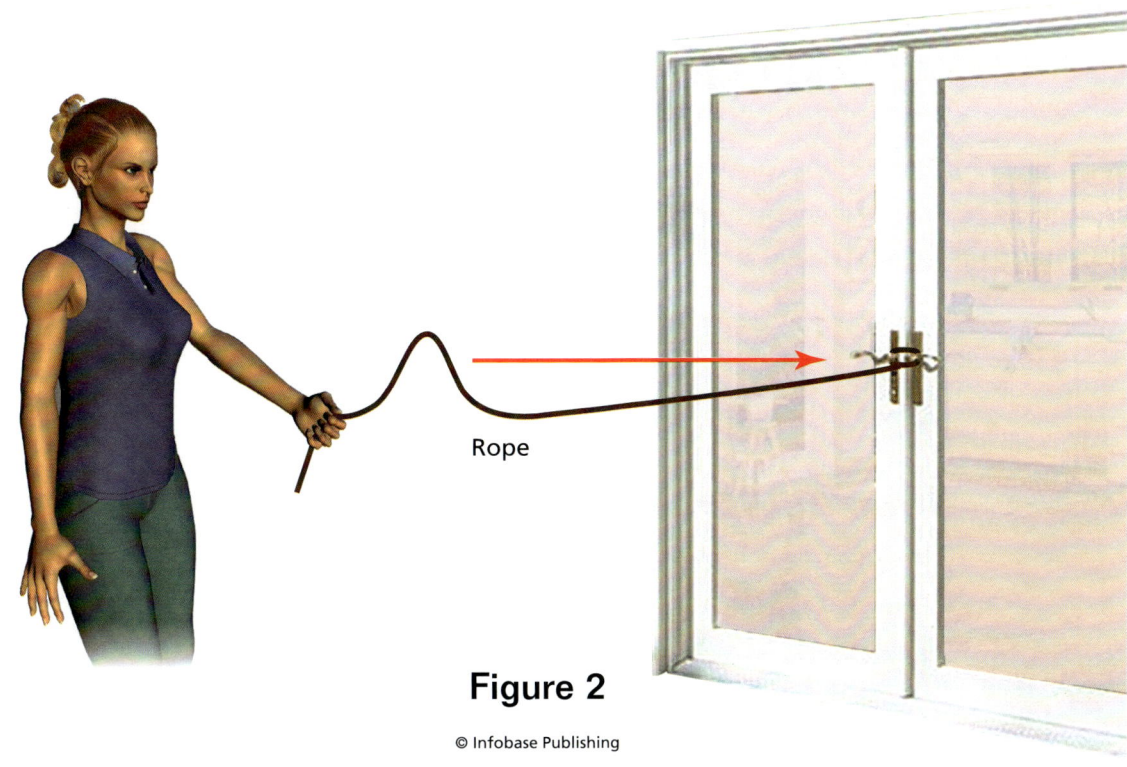

Figure 2

© Infobase Publishing

4. Allow the rope to stop moving. Repeat Step 3, but snap the end of the rope twice each second. Watch how the pattern in the rope changes and record your observations on the data chart.

Data Table 1	
Action	**Description of Waves**
Single small snap	
Single large snap	
One snap per second	
Two snaps per second	

Analysis

1. How did wave height in the first part of Step 2 compare with the wave height in the second part of Step 2?
2. How did the spacing of the waves in Step 3 compare with those in Step 4?
3. Based on your observations, how does increasing the energy affect the amplitude of the waves?
4. Based on your observations, how does increasing the frequency affect the wavelength of a wave?

What's Going On?

The size and shape of a wave are controlled by the amount of energy the wave carries and the frequency of the energy pulses. When you snap the end of the rope gently, the height of the wave is rather small. This is because the amount of energy used to displace the rope is small. Increasing the energy increases the height of the wave and its amplitude. The larger the amplitude of a wave, the more energy it carries.

The frequency of a wave is reciprocal to the wavelength. In other words, the higher the frequency, the shorter the length of the wave that is produced. When the frequency of a wave increases, the speed (or velocity) of the wave does not change. Because of this relationship, the increase in frequency is balanced by the decrease in wavelength. When you snapped the rope twice per second, you increased the frequency of the motion. The waves produced in the rope should have gotten shorter.

Our Findings

1. The height of the wave in Step 2 should have been greater than in Step 1.
2. The waves in Step 4 should have been closer together than in Step 3.
3. Increasing the energy increases the amplitude of the wave produced.
4. Increasing the frequency decreases the wavelength.

THE NATURE OF SOUND WAVES

Light waves, water waves, and even a wave cheer are examples of what scientists call **transverse waves**. In a transverse wave, the direction of the vibrations is at right angles to the direction that the wave travels. In other words, when the particles move up and down, the wave moves from side to side. Sound waves are different. A sound wave is an example of a **longitudinal wave.** In longitudinal waves, the vibrations and the waves move in the same direction. In **Experiment 3:** *Making Longitudinal Waves*, you and a friend will use a Slinky® to discover how a longitudinal wave travels.

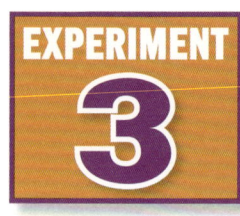

EXPERIMENT 3: Making Longitudinal Waves

Topic

How does the motion of a longitudinal wave differ from a transverse wave?

Introduction

When a sound wave moves out from a vibrating object, the material that it passes through vibrates. Because these vibrations are in the same direction that the wave travels, scientists call this a longitudinal wave. This is different from a light wave, which is a transverse wave. In a transverse wave, the particles vibrate at right angles to the direction that the wave travels. Like transverse waves, longitudinal waves can vary in frequency, amplitude, and wavelength. Because the vibrations are in the same direction of the wave motion, a longitudinal wave looks different. In this experiment, you will use a special type of spring to make a model of a sound wave to see how its motion is different from that of a transverse wave.

Time Required

45 minutes

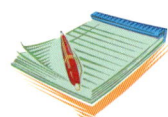

Materials

- Slinky® spring or 6-ft-long (2-m) piece of coiled telephone cord
- clear area on an uncarpeted floor about 10 ft (3 m) long
- person to assist you

Safety Note No special safety precautions are needed for this activity. Please review and follow the safety guidelines before proceeding.

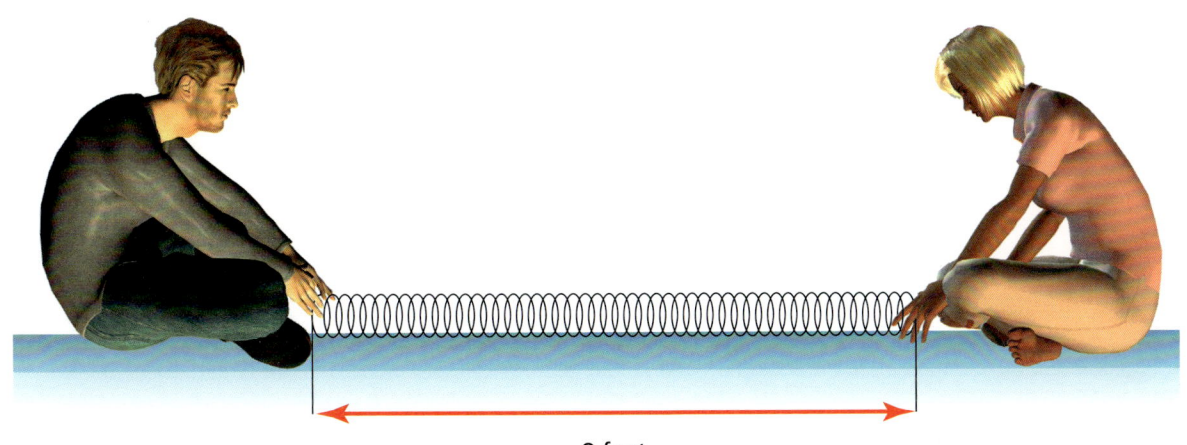

Figure 1

© Infobase Publishing

Procedure

1. Sit or kneel on the floor and hold on to one end of the Slinky® or telephone cord. Have your assistant hold onto the other end and sit or kneel about 8 ft (2.5 m) away from you (see Figure 1). Allow the spring to rest on the floor. The coils of the spring should be slightly stretched and not bunched up.
2. Tell your assistant to hold tightly to the spring while you give it one sharp jerk to the left. Observe the motion of the spring.
3. Allow the spring to stop moving and hold it straight again. While holding the end of the spring, pinch together five coils of the spring between your thumb and a finger so they are bunched together at your end. While still holding the end of the spring, release the five coils and observe the motion of the spring. Compare it to the motion of the spring in Step 2.
4. Repeat Step 3, but this time, pinch together 10 coils of the spring and then let it go. Observe the motion of the spring and compare it to the motion in Step 3.

Analysis

1. When you moved the spring from side to side, which direction did the wave travel? What type of wave is this?
2. When you pinched five coils together in Step 3 and let them go, how did the spring move? How did this compare with the motion in Step 2?

3. How did the motion of the spring in Step 3 compare with the motion of the spring in Step 1? What property of the wave did you change?

What's Going On?

When an object such as a tuning fork vibrates in the air, the energy of that motion moves out in all directions in a series of longitudinal waves. If you hit a tuning fork, the tines of the fork will begin to vibrate, creating sound waves. When the tines of the fork move, they push against the surrounding air, squeezing the molecules together. This outward push is known as a **compression**. When the tines move back together, the surrounding air molecules spread out. This opposite motion is called a **rarefaction**. When the tines move out again, another compression happens and the cycle continues until the fork stops vibrating.

In this experiment, compressing the coils of the springs and releasing them provided a good model for the motion of a vibrating tuning fork. The distance between the start of one compression and the next compression is one wavelength. Figure 2 shows what this looks like.

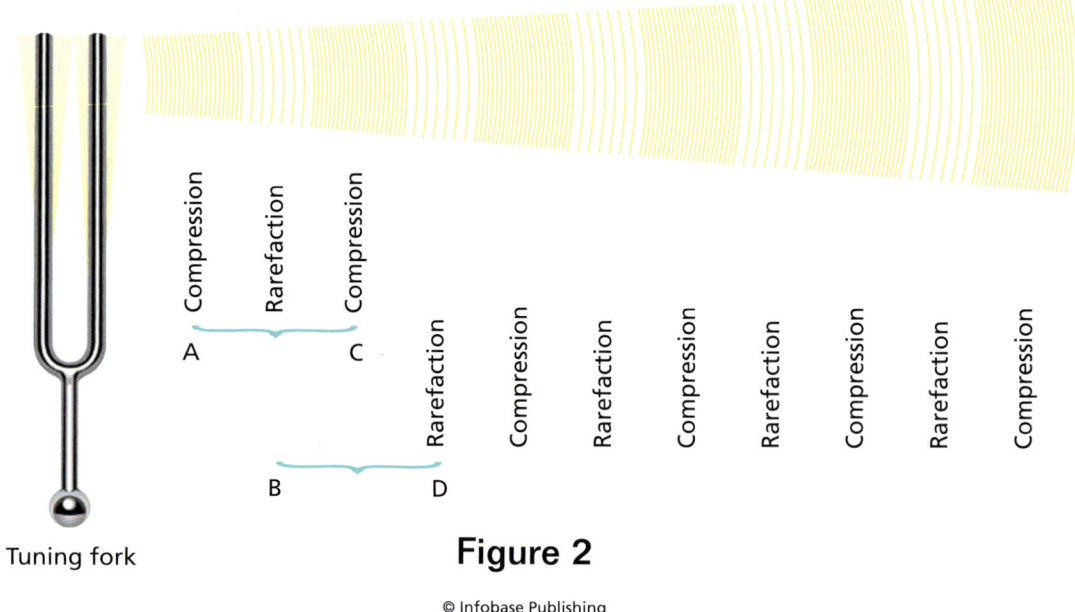

Tuning fork

Figure 2

© Infobase Publishing

Our Findings

Analysis

1. When the spring was moved from side to side, the wave traveled back and forth along the length of the spring. This motion is a transverse wave.
2. When the coils of the spring were compressed and released, the motion was along the length of the spring. This motion is a longitudinal wave.
3. When a greater number of coils were compressed and released, the wave traveled further along the spring because it had more energy. The wave had a larger amplitude.

REFLECTING ON A WAVE

If you have ever stood along the shore of an ocean or large lake, you've probably noticed that when waves strike an object along the water's edge, they don't just stop. In some cases, the waves will bounce off, or reflect. Water waves aren't the only type of wave that can reflect off surfaces. When you look into a mirror and see your own reflection, the image that you see is the result of a double reflection. Light waves bouncing off your face hit the mirror and reflect off it back to you. Sound waves can also be reflected. When you hear an echo, you are hearing sound waves bouncing off an object some distance away and returning to your ears a split second later. In **Experiment 4: *Reflecting Sound Waves***, you will experiment with reflecting sound waves off different surfaces to see how surfaces affect the sound of music.

EXPERIMENT 4

Reflecting Sound Waves

Topic
How do reflected sound waves help to alter the sound of a musical instrument?

Introduction
When musical instruments produce sounds, the waves travel in all directions. Sometimes these sound waves reflect or bounce off a surface, causing them to change direction. Over the years, scientists have discovered that by changing the size, shape, and composition of a reflecting surface, they also can alter the sound of musical instruments that are played near them. This is particularly important in concert halls and theaters. In this activity, you are going to test to see how the shape of a surface and the material from which it is made can affect the sound produced by a musical device.

Time Required
45 minutes

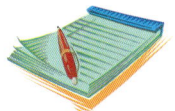

Materials

- rectangular piece of cardboard, poster board, or oak tag about 3 ft x 2 ft (100 cm x 60 cm)
- towel that is big enough to cover the cardboard
- portable radio, tape player, or other device with a speaker
- yardstick or meterstick
- large table
- quiet room
- person to assist you

30 MUSIC

> **Safety Note** No special safety precautions are needed for this activity. Please review and follow the safety guidelines before proceeding.

Procedure

1. Place the musical device on the table and turn it on so that the volume is moderately low. Turn the device so the speaker is facing away from you. Stand about 3 ft (1 m) behind the device and listen to how loud the sound is.

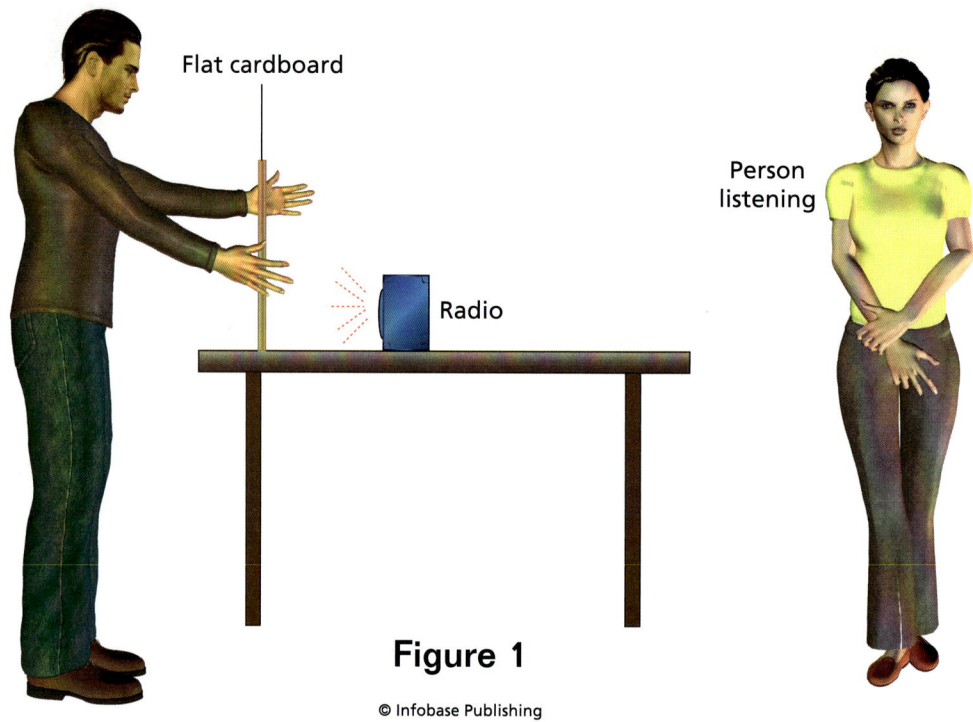

Figure 1

© Infobase Publishing

2. Continue standing in the same position. Have your assistant move to the other side of the table so they are standing opposite you. Have your assistant take the large piece of cardboard and stand it on edge about 1 ft (30 cm) behind the musical device. The speaker should be projecting directly into the cardboard. It should look like Figure 1. Listen to the sound of the musical device with the cardboard in place and compare it with the sound when the cardboard was not behind it. Ask your assistant to remove and put back the cardboard several times, so you can hear any sound difference.

3. Repeat Step 2. This time, ask your assistant to cover the front surface of the cardboard with the large towel. The musical device should project into the towel. Have your assistant take the towel on and off the cardboard several times. Compare the sound with and without the towel.

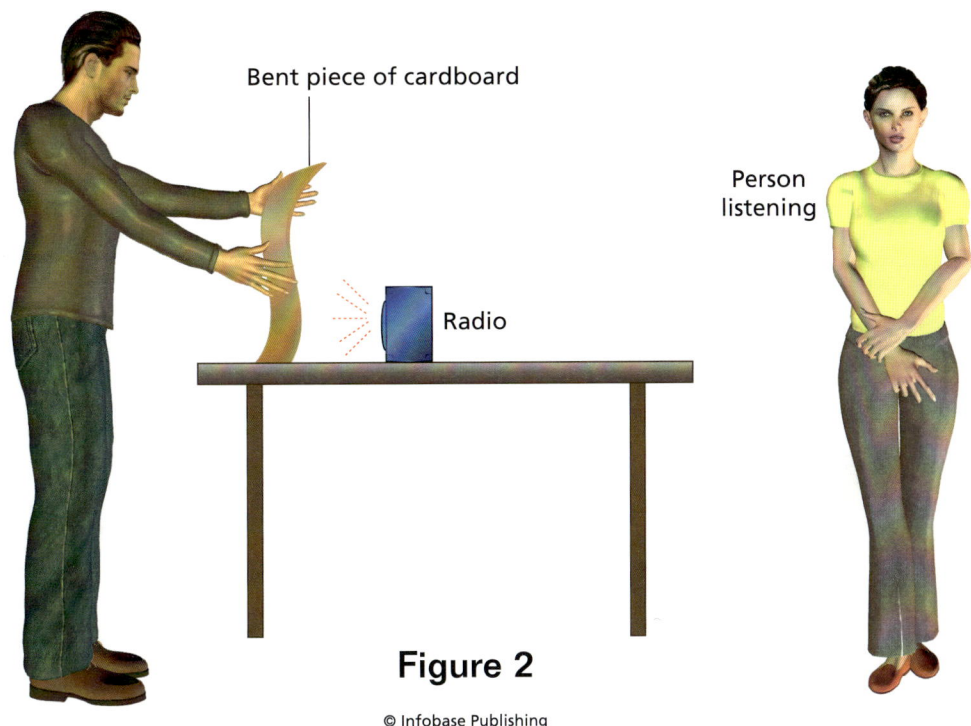

Figure 2
© Infobase Publishing

4. Ask your assistant to remove the towel from the cardboard. Repeat Step 2. This time, have your assistant carefully bend the edges of the cardboard toward you (as in Figure 2), so that the cardboard is now curved. Compare the sound produced with the curved cardboard to the sound produced with the flat cardboard. Have your assistant bend and straighten the cardboard several times so that you can make the sound comparison.

Analysis

1. How did the volume of the music without the cardboard behind the device compare with the volume when the flat piece of cardboard was behind it?
2. How was the music different when the cardboard behind the device was covered in a towel, compared with when the cardboard was bare?
3. How did the music sound when the cardboard behind the device was flat, compared with when the cardboard was bent?

What's Going On?

If you have ever visited a concert hall or been to an outdoor band shell, you've probably noticed that these structures are designed differently than regular buildings. They are designed to help project the music out to the audience. Under normal conditions, when a musician produces a note, the sound waves travel in all directions. As the waves travel, they tend to lose energy. The farther you are from the musician, the quieter the sound will be. In order to maximize the sound coming from the stage, concert halls use certain materials and design elements to reflect additional sound waves out toward the audience. In most concert halls, the ceiling near the stage and the walls on either side are made from hard materials, such as wood or plaster. These materials tend to reflect sound waves better than soft materials do. This is why, in your experiment, the cardboard covered with the towel led to softer sound than the one that was bare.

In addition to using hard materials, acoustic engineers also are concerned about the angles at which the sound waves travel after they reflect off a surface. By curving the wall and ceiling behind and above the stage, the sound waves are focused toward the audience in front. That's why, in your experiment, the curved piece of cardboard produced a louder sound than the flat piece of cardboard. This design feature is especially true for outdoor band shells and is why the world-famous opera house in Sydney, Australia has such an unusual shape.

Our Findings

Analysis

1. The music should have gotten louder when the cardboard was placed behind the device.
2. When the towel covered the cardboard, the music should have been softer than when the cardboard was bare.
3. Bending the cardboard should have made the sound louder than when the cardboard was flat.

AMPLITUDE AND LOUDNESS

In **Experiment 2:** *How Vibration Speed and Size Affect Waves*, you saw how snapping the rope with a greater amount of force or energy created a bigger wave. The part of the wave that shows how much energy it has is called the amplitude. The larger the amplitude of a wave, the more energy it has. In the case of sound waves, the amplitude is directly related to the volume or loudness of the sound. A sound wave with a large amplitude produces a loud sound. A wave with a small amplitude produces a soft sound.

When musicians play their instruments, controlling the amplitude of the wave that is produced is critical. Musicians have different amounts of control over how loud their instruments are. In many cases, the instrument itself will control how loud it can be played. In **Experiment 5:** *Controlling Instrument Volume*, you will test to see what factors control the amplitude of the sound waves created by a simple percussive instrument.

EXPERIMENT 5

Controlling Instrument Volume

Topic
What factors control how loud an instrument is?

Introduction
Several things control the loudness of a musical instrument. Sound is a form of mechanical energy. So changing the amount of energy used to play an instrument will affect how loud that instrument is. But energy alone does not always control the volume (amplitude) of a musical note. Some instruments are naturally loud, while others are soft. In this activity, you test to see what factors help to control the loudness of percussive instruments. Percussive instruments are those that are played by hitting them.

Time Required
45 minutes

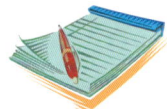

Materials

- large wooden spoon or drumstick
- large metal mixing bowl or pot
- small metal mixing bowl or pot
- small empty metal coffee can with one end removed
- 1 12-in. (30-cm) round balloon
- ruler
- 2 large rubber bands
- scissors
- 20 grains of uncooked rice

> **Safety Note** No special safety precautions are needed for this activity. Please review and follow the safety guidelines before proceeding.

Procedure

1. Use the scissors to cut the valve off the end of the balloon. You will be left with a curved sheet of rubber. Stretch the rubber sheet over the open end of the coffee can and wrap the two rubber bands around the top rim of the can to secure the balloon. The can should look like Figure 1.

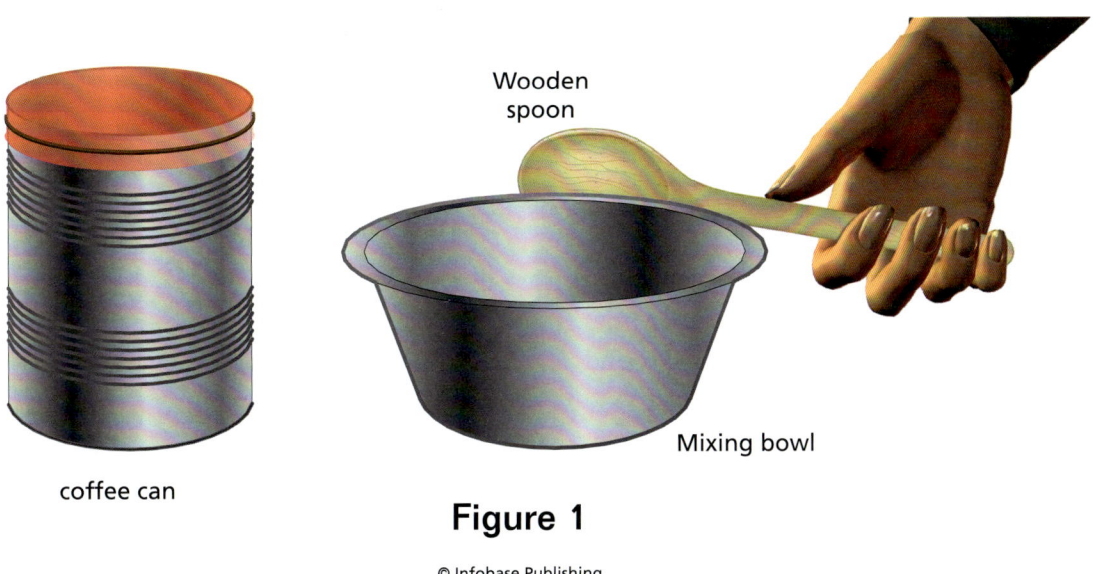

Figure 1

2. Place about 10 grains of rice on top of the balloon. Using one finger, tap the balloon gently and observe what happens to the rice. Now tap the balloon harder. Be careful not to tear the rubber. Observe what happens to the rice this time.

3. Place the coffee can on top of a sturdy table. Place the small mixing bowl next to it so that the top rim is exactly 6 in. (15 cm) away from the can. Using the wooden spoon or drumstick, gently strike the rim of the mixing bowl and listen to the sound it makes. Observe what happens to the rice on the can when you hit the bowl.

4. Repeat Step 3, but hit the bowl much harder. Make sure that the bowl is still 6 in. (15 cm) from the can, and be careful not to knock the bowl into the can. Listen to what happens to the volume of the sound from the bowl, and observe what happens to the rice.

5. Repeat Steps 3 and 4 again, but use the larger mixing bowl. Set the rim of the larger mixing bowl 6 in. (15 cm) from the can. Listen to the volume

of the sound produced this time and observe what happens to the rice on the coffee can.

Analysis

1. What happened to the rice on the top of the can when you hit the balloon with your finger? What happened when you hit it harder? Why?
2. What happened to the rice on the can when you hit the small mixing bowl softly, and then more firmly? Why?
3. What happened to the rice on the can when you hit the large mixing bowl? How did it compare with the smaller mixing bowl?
4. Based on the results of the experiment, which two factors control how loud a percussive instrument is?

What's Going On?

Musical instruments produce sounds in different ways. In instruments such as guitars and pianos, vibrating strings produce sound. Woodwinds, such as clarinets, have a vibrating reed. In brass instruments, such as trumpets, the vibrating lips of the musician produce the sound. In percussive instruments, such as drums and bells, the vibrations come from the surface of the object being hit. For most instruments, the more energy that is used to cause the vibration, the louder the sound will be, and the greater the amplitude of the sound wave. A guitar string that is plucked hard will make a louder sound than one plucked softly. In wind instruments, the harder the musician blows, the louder the note. In percussive instruments, this is easy to see. Hitting a drum forcefully will almost always produce a louder sound than hitting the same drum softly. Increasing the energy of vibration produces a louder sound because an increase in energy means that the vibrating object moves more air. The greater the amount of air set in motion, the larger the amplitude of the sound wave and the louder the sound produced.

Some instruments have a limit to their loudness, no matter how much energy is put into them. A triangle always will sound soft, no matter how hard you hit it. A piccolo will never be as loud as a trumpet, no matter how hard the musician blows. This is because these instruments are so small that they can never move a great deal of air. Large instruments will tend to make louder sounds, because they are designed to move large amounts of air when they vibrate. For this reason, it's difficult to play a gong or tuba very softly. The very act of playing these instruments sets so much air vibrating that they will usually sound loud.

Our Findings

Analysis

1. When you hit the balloon on the can with your finger, the rice bounced up and down because the balloon vibrated. Hitting it harder made the rice bounce more because there is more energy.
2. Hitting the bowl caused the rice to vibrate on the can. The sound wave produced by the bowl traveled through the air to the surface of the balloon, setting it in motion. Hitting the bowl softly made the balloon vibrate a small amount. Hitting it hard made the rice vibrate more because the sound wave was bigger.
3. Hitting the large mixing bowl caused the rice to vibrate more than hitting the small mixing bowl. The sound produced by the large mixing bowl was louder.
4. The volume of a percussive instrument is controlled by how hard it is hit and the size of the vibrating surface.

FREQUENCY AND PITCH

Musical notes have two separate parts to them. As we just discovered, the amplitude of a sound wave controls the loudness of the sound. The sound wave itself is created by a vibrating object. A second critical component of every note is the **pitch**. The pitch of a sound has nothing to do with throwing a baseball. It is a measure of how high or low a note is. The pitch of a sound is controlled by the frequency of the vibrations. In **Experiment 6:** *How Speed of Vibrations Affects Pitch of Sound*, you will test to see how the speed at which the air vibrates affects the pitch of the note that it produces.

EXPERIMENT 6
How Speed of Vibrations Affects Pitch of Sound

Topic
How does the speed of a vibration affect the pitch of a sound?

Introduction
When an object vibrates in the air, it produces a sound. These vibrations move through the air as pulses of energy called sound waves. The frequency of a sound wave describes how often the individual air particles vibrate back and forth. Wave frequency controls the pitch of a sound. Pitch is a way of describing how high or low a particular sound is. A piccolo has a high-pitched sound, while a tuba has a low-pitched sound. In this activity, you will test to see how changing the frequency of a vibration affects the pitch of a sound.

Time Required
30 minutes

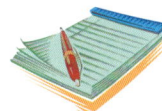

Materials
- 10 ft (3 m) rope (clothesline will do)
- safety glasses or goggles
- a clear, open space
- plastic ruler
- table or similar sturdy surface

Safety Note Make sure that when you swing the rope, nothing breakable and no other people are nearby. No other special safety precautions are needed for this activity. Please review and follow the safety guidelines before proceeding.

Procedure

1. Take one end of the rope and tie three or four knots in it. Put on the safety glasses and stand in the middle of a large open area. Make certain that there are no people or objects within 10 ft (3 m) of you.

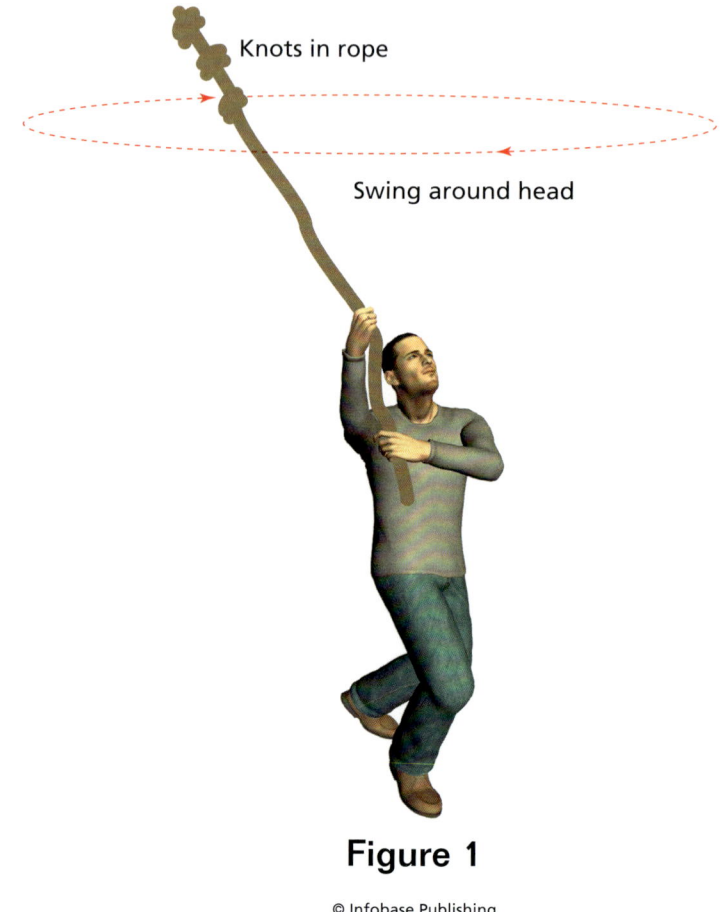

Figure 1

© Infobase Publishing

2. In one hand, firmly grasp the end of the rope without the knots. Begin slowly swinging the other end of the rope around your head. Figure 1 shows what this should look like. Listen to the sound that the rope makes as you swing it.

3. Gradually increase the speed at which you swing the rope. As you speed up, listen for any changes in the sound of the rope. Then, gradually slow down again until the rope comes to a stop. Listen for any changes in the sound as the rope slows down.

4. Put the rope down and pick up the ruler. Lay it on a table so that about half hangs over the edge and the other half is on the table. Hold the ruler down with one hand, and with the other hand strike the free end so that it vibrates up and down. Figure 2 shows how this should look.

Figure 2

5. Watch the speed of the vibrations of the ruler and listen to the sound that it makes. As you strike the ruler again, slide it onto the table so that the vibrating end becomes shorter. Listen to the sound it makes and observe what happens to the speed of the vibrations.

Analysis

1. What happened to the frequency of the vibrations as you increased the speed of the swinging rope?
2. What happened to the pitch of the sound as you increased the speed of the rope? What happened to the pitch as you decreased the speed?
3. What happened to the frequency of the vibrations of the ruler as you made the vibrating end of the ruler shorter? How did this affect the pitch of the sound that the ruler produced?
4. Based on your observations, what is the relationship between the frequency of a vibration and the pitch of a sound?

What's Going On?

As the frequency of a sound wave increases, the pitch of the sound that is produced gets higher. As the frequency of a sound wave increases, the waves produced by the vibrations get shorter. This can be seen with the vibrating ruler. As the length of the vibrating end decreased, the distance that the ruler moved back and forth also decreased, and the pitch got higher.

Our Findings

Analysis

1. Swinging the rope faster made the frequency of the vibrations increase.
2. As the rope moved faster, the pitch of the sound got higher. As the rope moved slower, the pitch got lower.
3. As the ruler got shorter, the frequency of the vibrations increased and the pitch of the sound got higher.
4. The greater the frequency of vibrations, the higher the pitch of the sound produced.

THE SOUND OF MUSIC

So far, we've covered the basics of how sounds are made, how they travel, and how different parts of a sound wave allow us to hear different things. By controlling the amplitude and pitch of a sound, musicians can create a variety of sounds that we hear as musical notes. By understanding how sound waves travel and reflect off surfaces, designers can build musical instruments that produce different sounds.

From here, we can explore how the science of sound is put to use in musical instruments. We also can learn how musicians use different sounds to make melodies that are pleasing to the ear. Before we can look at the way modern music is made, we will take a step back in time and see how this art form we call music got its start.

2

Early Music Makers

Music is not a modern invention. It is something that humans have been practicing for a very long time. We cannot know just how long, though, because back in the Paleolithic Age, or Stone Age, people did not have written languages. There are no records to tell us if they were playing musical instruments. Also, the first musical instruments looked nothing like the ones we have today. The first musical instruments, like the first tools and weapons, were simple objects made of wood, stone, and bone. In fact, the first musical instruments may have been tools and weapons that were modified to make certain sounds.

ANIMAL IMITATORS

Many scientists believe that before people actually built musical instruments, they probably made music using various body parts, just as other animals do. Singing, chanting, whistling, and clapping can be done without the use of additional objects. Before humans started composing music of their own, they may have started their musical inventions by imitating animal songs. Many animals—including birds, wolves, whales and insects—communicate with sound. Some animal songs may sound like random noise, but others have melodies and rhythms. Using sounds produced with their mouths, early humans easily could have imitated animal songs, putting their own twist on them to make them their own. In **Experiment 7:** *Controlling the Pitch of Sound with Your Mouth*, you will test to see how changing the shape of your mouth allows you to produce a variety of sounds that can be turned into simple songs.

EXPERIMENT 7
Controlling the Pitch of Sound with Your Mouth

Topic
How does the shape of your mouth control the pitch of a sound?

Introduction
Like many other animals, humans can use their mouths to make a variety of sounds that can be turned into music. In this activity, you will discover how to produce musical notes by changing the shape of your mouth and moving your tongue.

Time Required
30 minutes

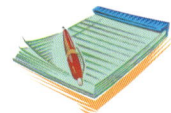

Materials
- your mouth
- a mirror

Safety Note No special safety precautions are needed for this activity. Please review and follow the safety guidelines before proceeding.

Procedure
1. Flick your tongue against the roof of your mouth so that you are making a clicking sound. Try changing the shape of your mouth to see how many different clicking sounds you can make.
2. Look in the mirror and watch the shape of your mouth when you make low-pitched clicking sounds and high-pitched clicking sounds. See if you can find a pattern between the shape of your mouth and the clicking sound produced. Record all observations in the data table.
3. Now, try whistling. Put your lips together and blow through them until you produce a whistle. Practice whistling different notes.

46 MUSIC

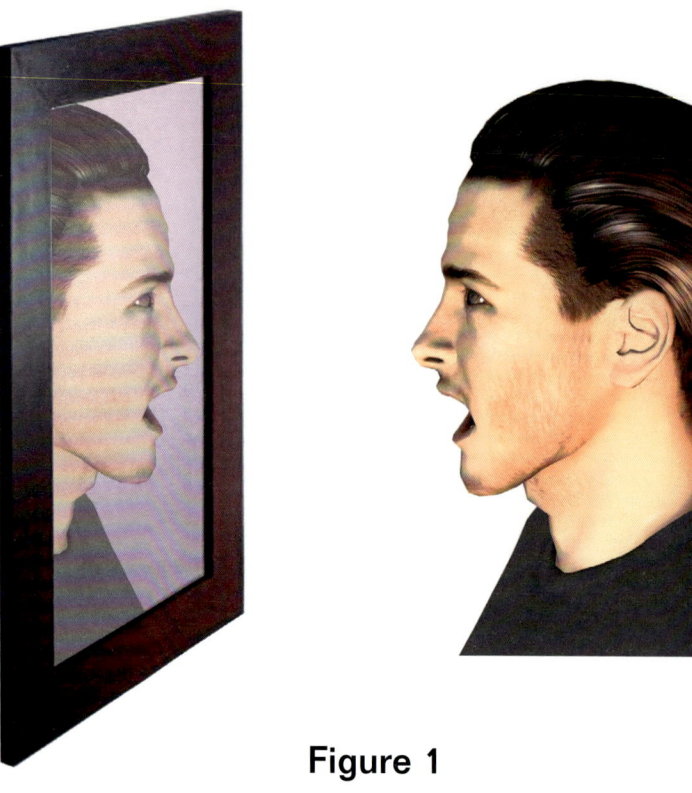

Figure 1

© Infobase Publishing

4. Look in a mirror and observe the shape of your lips when you whistle high-pitched notes and low-pitched notes. See if you can find a pattern between the shape of your lips and the pitch of the note you whistle.

Data Table 1	
Sound	**Shape of Mouth or Lips**
Low-pitched click	
High-pitched click	
Low-pitched whistle	
High-pitched whistle	

Analysis

1. How did the shape of your mouth change to produce high- and low-pitched clicks?
2. When you whistle, what part of your mouth creates the vibrations?
3. What did you have to do to whistle a high-pitched note?

What's Going On?

Changing the shape of your mouth and lips allows you to make different sounds because the shape controls the movement of air. When you produce a clicking sound, your tongue causes the roof of your mouth to vibrate like the head of a drum. These vibrations cause the air in your mouth to vibrate. When you open your mouth and stretch it wide, you are making the air space small and narrow. This causes the vibrations to speed up, producing a high-pitched sound. When you close your mouth and make it round in shape, you increase the volume of air held in your mouth. This causes the vibrations to slow down, producing a low-pitched sound.

When you whistle, the vibrations that produce the sound come from your lips vibrating. The size of your mouth's opening controls how fast the air vibrates. A smaller opening will cause the air to move faster, which causes the lips to vibrate faster. The faster the vibrations, the higher the sound produced.

Our Findings

Analysis

1. Low-pitched clicks are produced when the mouth is round. High-pitched clicks are made when the mouth is stretched wide.
2. When you whistle, your lips do the vibrating.
3. High-pitched whistles are produced when the opening between the lips is very small.

SING A SIMPLE SONG

When you whistle a tune, the shape of your mouth and lips allows you to control the pitch of the notes. When it comes to humming and singing, however, things are more complex. The shape of your mouth still plays a very important role, but the musical notes come from a different place. In **Experiment 8: *Controlling Vocal Cords***, you will discover how your voice box works to allow you to sing a range of musical notes.

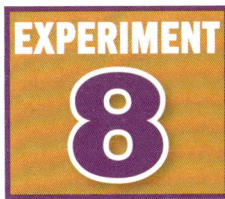

EXPERIMENT 8: Controlling Vocal Cords

Topic

How does controlling your vocal cords allow you to produce different musical notes?

Introduction

A large part of human speech is controlled by a complex structure located in our throats called the larynx, or voice box. Inside the voice box are fibrous membranes called vocal cords. They not only make speech possible, but also allow us to sing, chant, and hum complex songs.

The larynx is like a hollow tube in the middle of the throat. It is attached to the top of the trachea, or windpipe. When we breathe, air passes through the

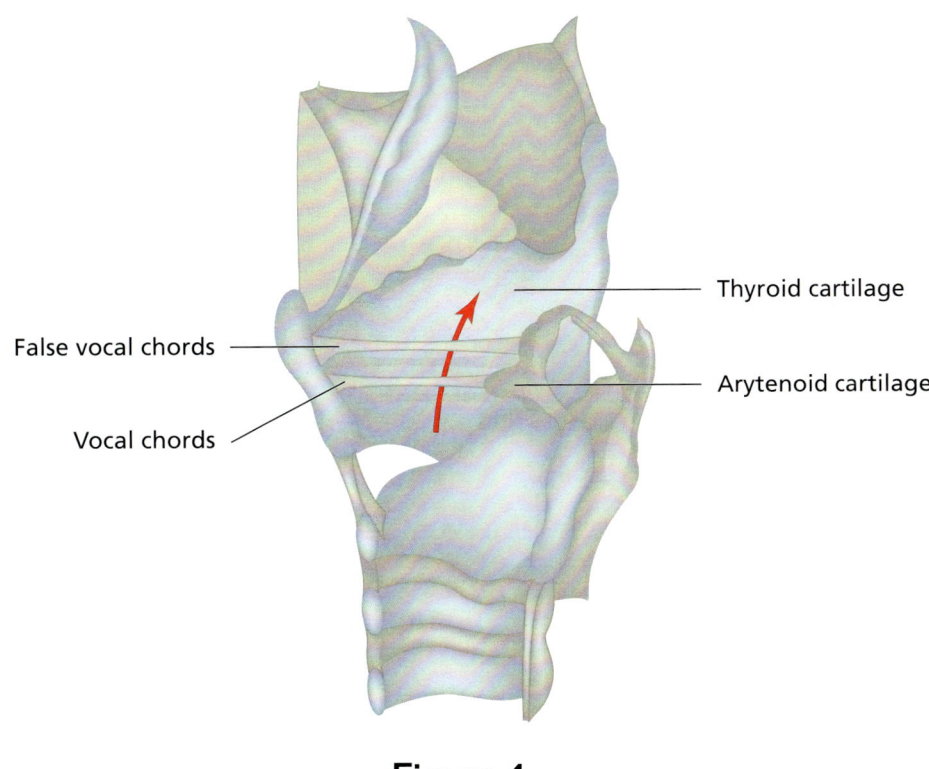

Figure 1

© Infobase Publishing

larynx on its way to the lungs. The larynx is made from plates of cartilage, held together by membranes and muscle. The front set of plates forms a lump that can be seen in the front of some people's throats. This lump is called the Adam's apple. In the center part of the voice box, the membrane lining the larynx narrows, forming two slitlike folds that stretch across the opening. These folds are the vocal cords. The vocal cords are attached to muscles that allow them to open, close, stretch, and tighten. In this activity, you will discover how to produce a range of musical notes by relaxing and tightening these muscles, and by changing the shape of your mouth.

Time Required

30 minutes

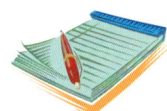

Materials

- your mouth, throat, and fingers
- mirror

Safety Note No special safety precautions are needed for this activity. Please review and follow the safety guidelines before proceeding.

Procedure

1. Rest one hand on your stomach, right below your rib cage. Gently rest two fingers of your other hand on the lump in your throat. Hum a low, steady note. Record what you feel in your throat and stomach.

2. Look in a mirror so that you can see your face and neck. With your hands in the same places, hum. Gradually raise the pitch of the note that you are humming. Record what you feel in your fingers and what you see in your throat as the note goes up.

3. Now it is time to do a little singing. Repeat the procedure you followed in Step 2, but instead of humming, sing a simple scale. Start at a low note. You can use the standard notes (do – re – mi – fa – so – la – ti – do), or make one up of your own. Observe the shape of your mouth as you sing each note, and record what you see.

4. Repeat Step 3. This time, keep your mouth wide open while you sing the same scale. Record what you see.

Analysis

1. When you placed your fingers on your throat, what did you feel when you began humming?
2. What happened to the muscles in your throat when the pitch of the note you were humming went from low to high?
3. When you sang the scale, what happened to the shape of your mouth as you changed each note?
4. What happened to your ability to sing different notes when you kept your mouth open?

What's Going On?

When you hum and sing different musical notes, your vocal cords make vibrations that cause sounds. This happens as air is forced from your lungs and through your windpipe. Your diaphragm—a muscle at the base of your rib cage—pushes the air out of your lungs. When you sing or speak, you should be able to feel your diaphragm moving. As the moving air passes by the vocal cords, they begin to vibrate. You can think of your vocal cords like stretched rubber bands. The tighter they get, the faster they vibrate, and the higher is the pitch of the sound they create. When you hum or sing up a scale, you can actually feel the muscles in your throat getting tighter as the vocal cords stretch.

The initial vibrations are created by the vocal cords, but specific sounds or musical notes are formed with the help of the mouth, lips, and tongue. As you change the shape of your mouth, the size of the air chamber through which the sound is moving also changes. It is extremely difficult to sing different musical notes while holding your mouth in just one position.

Our Findings

Analysis

1. When you hum with your fingers on your throat, you should feel a buzzing in your fingers. This is the vibration of your vocal cords.
2. As you changed pitch from low to high, the muscles in your throat should have gotten tighter. While that was happening, your vocal cords also were stretching.

3. As you sing different notes, the shape of your mouth changes.
4. If you try to sing a musical scale with your mouth held open, the sounds of the notes will not be as distinct.

EARLY INSTRUMENTS

Scientists still do not agree on how the first musical instruments looked and when they were developed. Some scientists believe that the first true musical instruments were a fairly recent development, dating back to around 60,000 years ago. Others believe that early humans were using some form of instrument as long as they have been using simple tools. If this is the case, music may date as far back as 2 million years ago! It is hard to pinpoint a time because many instruments may not have been preserved. Also, many of the first musical instruments probably also had other uses. This would make them hard to recognize as musical instruments. Scientists working on an ancient archaeological site today would have a difficult time figuring out if certain objects were used for their sound, or were used only as tools.

Though we can't be certain, many historians believe that the first instruments were probably percussive. People play percussive instruments by striking, shaking, or rubbing them. Some modern examples are drums, gongs, and cymbals. It's easy to imagine how these may have been created. People using stone or bone hammers to crack nuts would have noticed that different materials made different sounds. If these sounds caught their interest, it's quite possible that they could have collected certain objects and used them to make primitive idiophones. An idiophone is an instrument that makes a sound when the entire surface vibrates. In **Experiment 9:** *Musical Wood Blocks*, you will discover how something as simple as a piece of wood could have been turned into a musical instrument.

EXPERIMENT 9

Musical Wood Blocks

Topic
How does the condition of a piece of wood control the sound that it makes when struck?

Introduction
Anyone who has hammered a nail into a board, or struck a tree branch with an axe, knows that wood makes a sound when you hit it. Some pieces of wood make a ringing sound. Others make a thud. Several factors control the type of sound that a piece of wood will make. In this activity, you will test to see how the condition of a piece of wood affects the sound that it makes.

Time Required
60 minutes

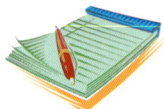

Materials
- hammer
- saw
- electric drill with ¼-in. bit
- gloves
- goggles or safety glasses
- tape measure or ruler
- pencil
- wooden 2 x 4 (approximately 5 cm x 10 cm), about 2 ft (60 cm) long
- bucket or dishpan filled with water
- brick or large stone
- three nails with large heads

- piece of heavy string about 3 ft (1 m) long
- scissors

Safety Note This activity requires adult supervision. Make certain that you and anyone near you are wearing goggles and work gloves during the preparation part of this activity. Please review and follow the safety guidelines.

Procedure

1. With the help of an adult, cut the 2 x 4 (approximately 5 cm x 10 cm) piece of wood into three pieces. Each piece should be exactly 6 in. (15 cm) long. When cutting the wood, wear gloves and safety glasses.
2. Hammer a nail into the end of each piece of wood so that about 1 in. (2 cm) of the nail is sticking out of the wood. Place one piece of wood off to the side. Place another piece in the bucket of water. Cover it with a brick or large stone so that it is completely submerged. Let it soak in the

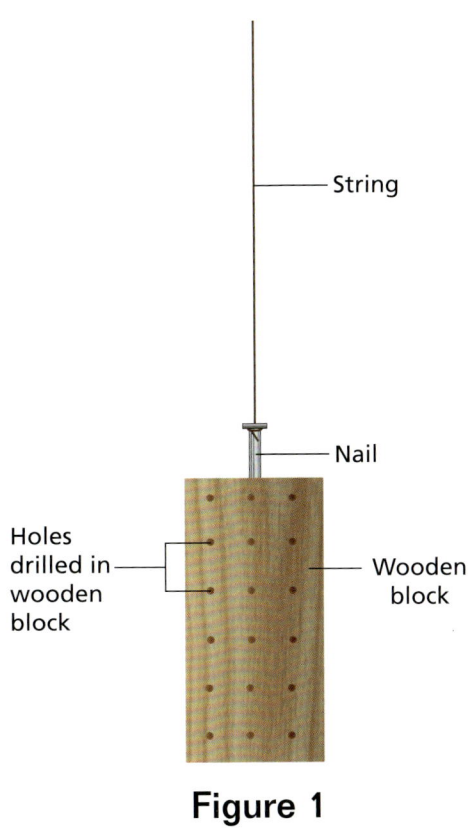

Figure 1

© Infobase Publishing

water for at least 45 minutes. Ask an adult to drill 15 to 20 holes all the way through the third piece of wood. When drilling, lay the piece of wood on top of a scrap piece of wood, so that you don't accidentally drill into the table.

3. After 45 minutes, take the wood out of the bucket. Cut the string into three equal pieces and tie one piece of string to the nail in each piece of wood. Test the strength of the knot by lifting each piece of wood by the string.

4. Pick up the dry piece of wood without the holes by its string so that it is hanging in the air. Using the wooden handle of the hammer, gently tap on the wood a few times and listen to the sound.

5. Repeat Step 4 with the other two pieces of wood. Compare the sounds that all three pieces make. Record all observations on the data table. Based on your observations, think about which physical property is affecting the sound that each piece of wood produces.

Data Table 1	
Condition of Wood	**Type of Sound Produced**
Dry without holes	
Dry with holes	
Wet without holes	

Analysis

1. Did all three pieces of wood produce the same sound? If not, how were they different?
2. Why did you need to use a single wooden 2 x 4 cut into sections?
3. Why did the pieces of wood have to be suspended from strings when you hit them?

What's Going On?

Many physical properties affect the sound that a piece of wood will make. These include the type of wood, its overall density, and how dry it is. In this experiment, you tested some of these variables by selecting a single piece of wood and cutting it into similar lengths. The wood that was soaked in the bucket was saturated with water. When it was struck, it vibrated poorly and made a dull sound. That's because the water in the wood cells absorbed some of the vibrations. The piece of wood with the holes had air passages, which reduced its ability to vibrate. The dry piece without the holes was solid throughout with very little moisture in it. This meant it was the best at transmitting sound waves.

Through trial and error, early humans easily could have made these same discoveries. They may not have known the technical explanation for why each piece of wood sounded the way it did. They quickly would have learned, however, to select only the pieces of wood that made particular sounds.

Our Findings

Analysis

1. Each piece of wood produced a different sound. The dry piece without holes produced a low tone that was sharp. The wet piece produced a low tone that was dull. The dry piece with the holes produced a dull note that was a bit higher pitched than the others.
2. All three pieces of wood had to come from the same source so that in doing the test, you could be certain that it was either the holes drilled in the wood or the water that was producing a change in the sound
3. The pieces of wood had to be suspended from string so that they would vibrate freely when they were hit with the hammer.

WIND SONGS

While it is quite likely that percussive instruments were the first ones developed by humans, wind instruments probably weren't too far behind. In nature, wind blowing through tree branches and grasses makes a wide range of sounds. People

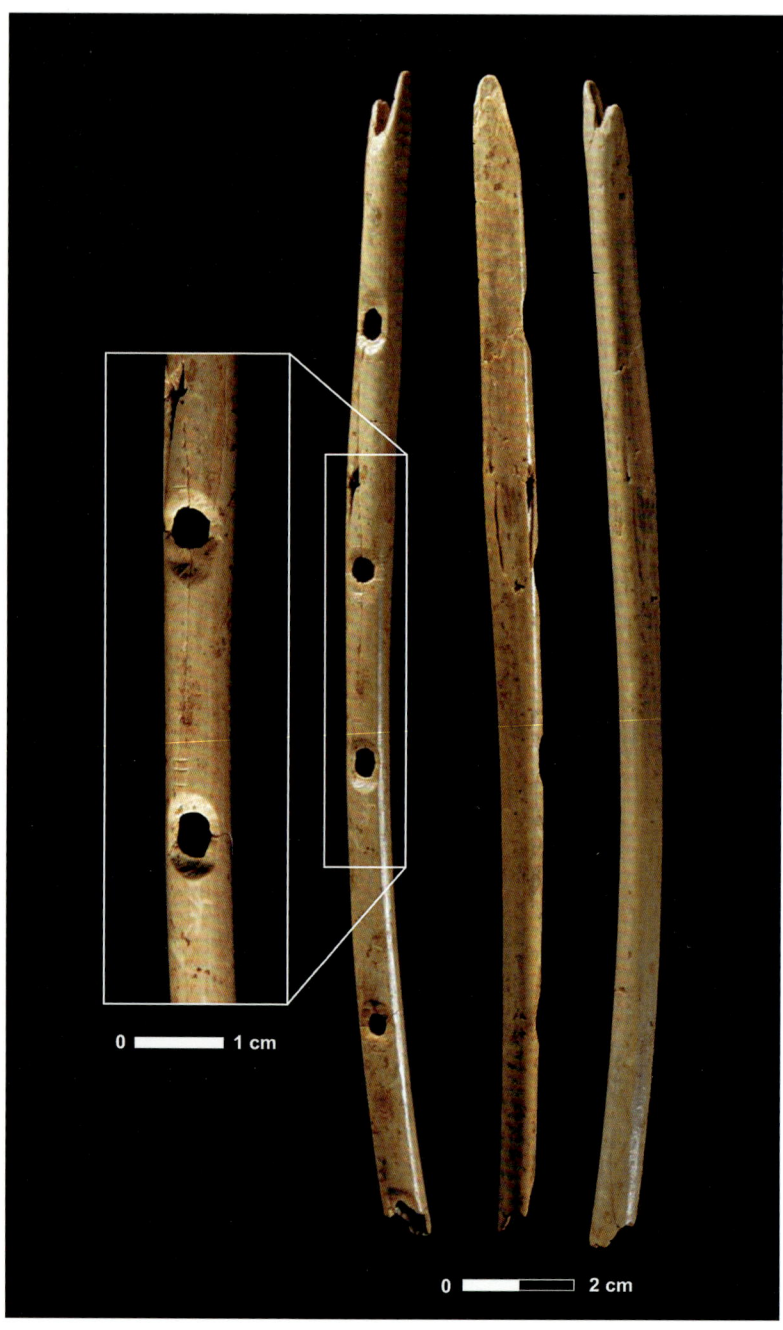

The earliest wind instrument to be discovered so far was this bone flute (seen from different angles) with five finger holes. The instrument, believed to be from the Paleolithic Era, also has two V-shaped indentations on one end, presumably for a person to blow into the instrument.

could have easily mimicked these. Blowing into a hollow tube could have given rise to primitive flutes and pipes.

Archaeologists still debate when the first wind instruments were developed. The earliest confirmed wind instrument is about 36,000 years old. It was discovered in Geissenklosterle, Germany. It is a simple bone flute, made from the hollow wing bone of a swan. The flute has a number of holes drilled in it, which would allow the person playing it to play different notes.

In 1995, Ian Turk, a paleontologist from Slovenia, discovered an artifact in a cave occupied by Neanderthals about 43,000 years ago. Turk claims it also is a simple flute. This one is made from the hollowed-out bone of a cave bear, and has four small holes in a row along one side. Some scientists believe this is a musical instrument. Others think it is merely the remains of someone's dinner, and that the holes are nothing more than tooth marks. There is probably no way to know for sure, but the fact remains that people have been making and playing wind instruments for a very long time. In **Experiment 10:** *Effect of Tube Length on Sound Pitch,* you will construct one of the oldest types of wind instruments using some modern materials.

EXPERIMENT 10
Effect of Tube Length on Sound Pitch

Topic
How does the length of a tube control the pitch of a sound?

Introduction
The simplest form of flute is nothing more than a hollow tube or pipe, played by blowing over the open end. It's similar to blowing over the open end of a soda bottle. Early pipes were made from hollowed-out wood, reeds, clay, and even stone. Panpipes are constructed by fastening together tubes of different lengths. This type of instrument has been in use for more than 2,000 years. Panpipes have been found all over the world. Modern panpipes are still played in South America, where they are used in the traditional music of Peru.

In this activity, you will build a set of simple panpipes using drinking straws to test the relationship between the length of a pipe and its pitch.

Time Required
45 minutes

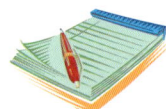

Materials
- 3 identical plastic drinking straws
- scissors
- ruler
- roll of cellophane tape

Safety Note No special safety precautions are needed for this activity. Please review and follow the safety guidelines before proceeding.

Procedure

1. Place the end of one of the straws on top of your lower lip. Hold the straw in the middle and blow across the open top so that you make a sound. Pretend you are blowing across the open end of a bottle. Figure 1 shows you how this should look.

Figure 1

© Infobase Publishing

2. Repeat Step 1, but use the thumb of your other hand to block the bottom of the straw. Do this several times, and compare the sound of the straw when the bottom is open to when it is closed.

3. Measure a second straw and use the scissors to cut it in half. Blow across the end of one half of the cut straw and compare the sound to the sound of the full-length, open straw. Use your thumb to block the bottom of the cut straw and listen to the sound again. Compare the sound of the closed half-straw to the open full straw.

4. Measure the third straw and cut it so that you have two pieces that are ¼ and ¾ of the original length. Blow into each piece and compare the sounds that they make with the bottoms open.

5. Lay the three pieces of straw next to the full-sized straw on a flat surface. The full straw should be first, followed by the ¾-length straw, then the ½-length straw, and finally the ¼-length straw. Line up the straws so that their top ends are even. Tape the straws together. The assembled pipes should look like Figure 2. You have now made a panpipe. Play it by sliding it back and forth across your lip while blowing into it.

62 MUSIC

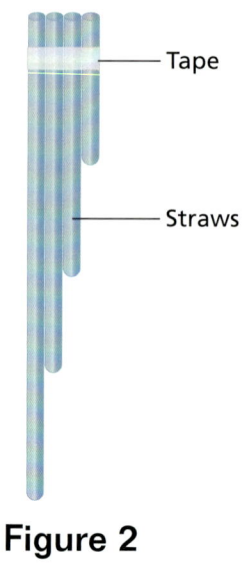

Figure 2

© Infobase Publishing

Analysis

1. What happened to the sound of the full-length straw when you opened and closed the end while blowing over it?
2. How did the sound of the straw that was cut in half compare to the full-length straw when the bottom was open? How did the half-straw sound when the bottom end was closed?
3. How did the sound of the ¼-length straw compare to the sound of the ¾-length straw? How did these sounds compare to the open full straw and open half-straw?
4. Based on your experiment, what is the relationship between the length of a straw and the sound it makes?
5. Why does closing the end of the straw cause the note to change?

What's Going On?

When you blow into a pipe, flute, or other wind instrument, the column of air that is trapped inside the tube produces sound. When the air flows through the tube, it produces a standing wave. The length of the wave is controlled by the length of the tube. The pitch of the sound (the note produced) is controlled by the frequency of the sound wave. High frequencies (many vibrations per second) produce high-pitched notes, while low frequencies produce low-pitched notes. Increasing the length of the tube increases the wavelength of the standing wave that is formed inside it.

Because longer waves vibrate at a lower frequency (fewer wavelengths per second), the pitch of a sound from a longer tube will be lower than sound from a short tube.

With wind instruments, there is a mathematical relationship between the length of the tube and the note that it produces. Cutting a tube in half will produce a note that is exactly one octave higher than the full tube. Doubling the length of a tube will produce a note that is exactly one octave lower. An octave is made up of eight full notes on the musical scale. A note that is an octave higher is the same note at the next higher pitch.

When you blow through an open tube, the vibrating air exits at the other end. If you close the bottom end of the tube, the air in the tube can exit only from the top end. As the sound wave moves inside the tube, it goes all the way to the bottom and returns to the top. This doubles the length of the wave, which cuts the frequency of the vibrations in half. The note produced will be one octave lower than the note produced in the open tube. Covering the bottom of the tube has the same effect as doubling the length of the tube.

Our Findings
Analysis

1. The sound made with the closed straw should have been lower than the sound made with the open straw. The closed straw should produce a note that is one octave lower than the open straw.
2. The sound made with the open half-straw should be one octave higher than the sound made with the open full straw. The closed half-straw should produce the same note as the open full straw.
3. The ¼-length straw should produce the highest note. The ¾-length straw should produce a note that is between the full straw and half-straw when the bottoms are open.
4. The longer the straw, the lower the note produced.
5. Closing the end of the straw makes the air move back up to the top opening, which has the same effect as doubling the length of the tube.

ROCKING IN RHYTHM

Until now, we have focused mostly on how individual sounds are made and how the loudness and pitch of different musical notes can be controlled. Before we end the discussion on the origins of music, it is important to look at one other critical part of all music: rhythm. Rhythm is not concerned with the production of individual notes. Instead, it has to do with how the notes are spaced. Rhythm controls the beat of the music and the timing of the notes. In fact, to make a rhythm, you don't even need an instrument. All you have to do is clap your hands, snap your fingers, or stamp your feet. For some musicians, the rhythm is more important than the musical notes. Without rhythm, music wouldn't be any fun to dance to, and hip-hop and rock and roll couldn't exist.

Music isn't the only thing with a rhythm. Anything that involves timing involves rhythm. Rhythm is a big part of nature. The seasons have a rhythm, and so do the tides. When people walk or run, they do so in a natural rhythm. Birds' wings have a rhythm when they fly, and fish tails move with a rhythmic pattern when they swim. Even when we speak, our words tend to follow a rhythm.

In **Experiment 11:** *Song Rhythm vs. Note Timing*, you'll explore the basics of rhythm in music and discover why the beat is an important part of any song.

EXPERIMENT 11: Song Rhythm vs. Note Timing

Topic

How does the rhythm of a song relate to the timing of the notes?

Introduction

Almost every piece of music has some type of rhythm. Rhythm is what determines the timing of the musical notes. Some forms of music don't even have a melody made up of notes. Instead, the "song" is nothing but a series of beats played on a variety of different rhythm instruments. In this activity, you will experiment with changing the rhythm of a simple song to see how it affects the timing of the song and the way the melody sounds.

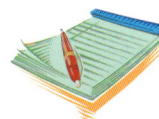

Time Required

45 minutes

Materials

- clock that measures seconds
- piano or electronic keyboard
- masking tape
- pencil

Safety Note No special safety precautions are needed for this activity. Please review and follow the safety guidelines before proceeding.

Procedure

1. Look at the drawing of the keyboard in Figure 1, showing which keys represent which musical notes. If you are familiar with a keyboard, you will recognize the notes. If you are not familiar with a keyboard, use the diagram

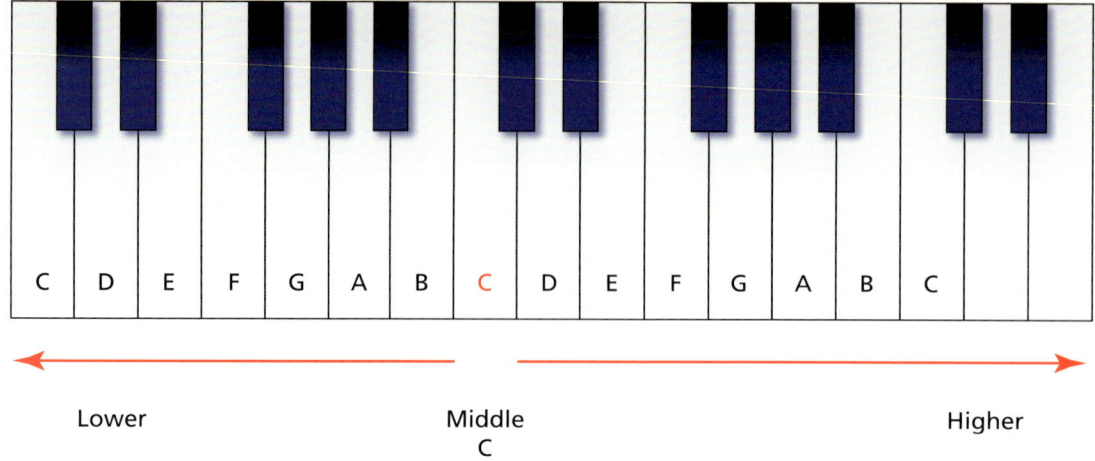

Figure 1

© Infobase Publishing

to locate the note "C" near the middle of your keyboard. Tear off a piece of tape and place it on the key. Use the pencil to label it "C". Now locate the "E" note—two white keys to the right of "C"—and label it. Next, locate the "G" note—two white keys to the right of "E"—and label it with tape.

2. Try playing the notes in the following order: C-C-E-E-G-G-E. Practice it a few times so that you get familiar with the pattern.

3. Using the clock as a guide, begin tapping your foot once each second. Continue this pace for about fifteen seconds. Each time you tap your foot counts as one beat.

4. Start tapping your foot once each second again and as you do, play the sequence of notes so that you give each note two beats. In other words, play a note on a beat, and then wait one second before playing the next note. Listen to the tempo of the song.

5. Repeat Step 4, but when you play the notes, give each note only one beat. Listen to the tempo of the song this time.

6. Repeat Step 4, but when you play the notes, alternate the number of beats between each note. Give the first "C" one beat, the second "C" two beats, the first "E" one beat, the second "E" two beats, and so on. Listen to the melody of the song as you play.

7. Repeat Step 4, but give each note a different number of beats so that the rhythm is random. Compare the melody of the song to the melodies you played in Steps 5 and 6.

Analysis

1. What happened to the tempo of the song when you went from two beats per note to only one beat per note?
2. What happened to the melody of the song when you changed the rhythm by alternating the number of beats for each note?
3. What happened to the melody of the song when you used a random rhythm?
4. Based on your observations, why role does the rhythm play in a song?

What's Going On?

Without rhythm, a song would be a random sequence of musical notes. It would sound strange and chaotic. The rhythm determines the timing of the notes and the pace at which they are played. The origin of the word *rhythm* is not easy to trace. It comes from the Greek word *rhythmos,* which in turn is related to the word *rhein,* which means "to flow." Rhythm controls the flow of the musical notes. A musical rhythm can be broken down into two parts. First is the beat, which is the actual pattern that the musical notes follow. The beat shows how the musical notes are played and the spacing between them. Individual notes can be held for any number of beats, including fractions of beats. The second part of rhythm is the tempo, which is the overall pace or speed. The tempo determines how fast the notes are played. By controlling the beat and the tempo of a melody, a musician can take the same set of notes and make it sound like very different songs.

Our Findings

Analysis

1. As you reduced the number of beats per note from two to one, the tempo of the song increased.
2. When you change the number of beats between notes, the music sounds different, though the notes are the same and are in the same sequence.
3. When you play a series of notes with a random rhythm, it becomes difficult to hear a melody.
4. In music, the rhythm controls both the tempo (speed) of the music, as well as the time spacing between the notes.

MATHEMATICAL MUSIC

By now, you have probably noticed that there are many connections between music and math. You discovered how changing the frequency of vibrations and the wavelength of a sound can change the pitch of a musical note, as well as how the length of a tube can change the frequency of vibrations. By experimenting with changing rhythms, you found that the timing of the musical notes are just as important as playing the notes themselves. As we continue, you will see many other places where mathematics and music come together. Because we are going to focus primarily on the science of music, there won't be much discussion of the math. Still, mathematics is the "language of science," so the two are almost impossible to separate. The next unit focuses on one of the greatest mathematicians of all time, and how his ideas about music helped shape the way it was played for thousands of years.

3

Instruments with Strings

The first two units covered some of the basic science of sound and the early development of music. Now we'll narrow the focus to concentrate on one class of instruments: the **chordophones**. A chordophone is a musical instrument that produces sound by a vibrating string. Chordophones are divided into five types that are based on how the string or strings attach to the instrument and how the strings are put into motion.

The lyre is one of the simplest types of chordophone. Its strings are stretched between two crossbars, which are supported by two arms. Lyres, which were common in ancient Egypt, were first used about 5,000 years ago. The harp appeared at about the same time as the lyre. It is similar to the lyre, but the strings run diagonally between the supports, instead of at right angles. Lyres are mostly used as ceremonial instruments today, but harps still are played in many orchestras.

Each instrument in the lute family has a neck with strings running over it. Each instrument also has a bridge, which holds the strings above the body of the instrument. This allows the strings to vibrate freely. Primitive lutes date back several thousand years, but other members of this group are quite popular today. Modern members of the lute family include the violin, cello, and guitar. If it were not for the development of the lute, many types of music—from stringed symphonies by Mozart to Metallica's heavy metal—would not be possible.

The most complex type of chordophone is the zither. In this instrument, the strings run parallel to each other for the entire length of the instrument. Bridges support the strings, allowing

The lyre (*left*) is the simplest of the chordophones, while the zither (*right*) is the most complex. A lyre has strings stretched between two crossbars, supported by two arms; the zither has strings that run the entire length of the soundboard. The lyre is usually held as it is played, while the zither is rested on the performer's knees or on a table.

them to vibrate freely. Depending on the design, zithers can be played by either plucking the strings or hitting the strings with a hammer. Many zithers have been modified to include a keyboard mechanism that activates the strings. These include harpsichords, as well as the most common type of zither: the piano.

The simplest and most ancient chordophone is the musical bow. The bow is typically a wooden rod with horsehairs stretched from one end to the other that it used in playing an instrument in the violin family. In **Experiment 12: *Creating Tension on a Vibrating String***, you will construct a musical bow and use it to discover how changing the tension of a string alters the pitch of a note.

Experiment 12

Creating Tension on a Vibrating String

Topic

How does the tension of a vibrating string control the pitch of the note that it produces?

Introduction

Over the years, people have produced many different stringed instruments. Most music historians believe that the first stringed instruments, or chordophones, were nothing more than simple bows. These date back thousands of years and were probably adapted from the bows that people used for hunting. These days, the main use of the bow in music is to play other stringed instruments, such as the violin and cello. Musical bows used in the past have been found all over the world, including Asia and the Americas. Today, they are still played in parts of Africa. Musical bows have evolved over the years to include devices that make them sound louder. In this activity, you will construct and play a simple musical bow to discover how it produces musical notes.

Time Required

30 minutes

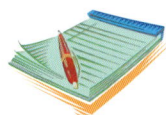

Materials

- yardstick, meterstick, or narrow piece of wood about 39 in. long, 1 in. wide, and ¼ in. thick (1 m long x 2 cm wide x ½ cm thick)
- ruler
- electric drill with ¼-inch bit
- safety glasses or goggles
- roll of kite string or package string
- scissors

72 MUSIC

> **Safety Note** This activity requires adult supervision. Make certain that you and anyone near you are wearing goggles when drilling the wood. Please follow the rest of the safety guidelines.

Procedure

1. Many yardsticks and metersticks have holes in their ends. If yours does, skip this step. Otherwise, ask an adult to drill a hole at each end of the stick you are using. Each hole should be about 1 in. (2 cm) from each end.
2. Thread the string through one of the holes and pull about 4 in. (10 cm) through the hole. Wrap the end of the string around the end of the wood a few times and then knot it so the string is secure (see Figure 1).

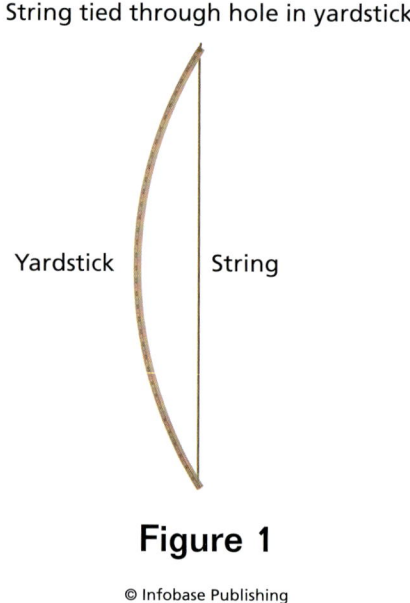

String tied through hole in yardstick

Yardstick   String

Figure 1

© Infobase Publishing

3. Unroll the string and lay it on top of the wood so that it stretches to the other end. Measure an additional 6 in. (15 cm) of string past the end of the wood and cut the string. Thread the cut end of the string through the open hole, making sure that the string stays on the same side of the wood. Gently bend the wood so that it makes a bow shape. Tie the string as you did at the other end. The completed bow should look like Figure 1.
4. Using your fingers, pluck the string and listen to the sound it makes. Be careful not to bend the bow as you are plucking the string.
5. Pluck the string again while pressing the two ends of the bow closer together. Observe what happens to the tightness of the string. Compare the sound of the bow to the sound it made in Step 4.

6. Next, gently pull the ends of the bow apart. Observe what happens to the tightness of the string. Pluck the string and compare the sound of the bow to the sounds produced in Steps 4 and 5.

7. By changing the tension of the bow, see how many different notes you can play. If the spirit moves you, see if you can pluck out a little tune!

Analysis

1. What is responsible for making the sound in the musical bow?
2. What happened to the tension of the string when you pushed the ends of the bow closer together? How did the sound of the bow change?
3. What happened to the tension of the string when you pulled the two ends of the bow farther apart? How did the sound of the bow change?
4. Based on your experiments, what can you say about the relationship between the sound produced by a vibrating string and its tightness?

What's Going On?

When you pluck a string on any chordophone, the string begins to vibrate, making a sound. Several factors affect the pitch of the note that a string makes. String tension is one of the most important. When a string is tight, it will vibrate faster than when it is loose. The tighter you make a string, the faster the wave moves along it. This increases the frequency of the sound waves it produces. Higher-frequency waves create a sound with a higher pitch, so the tighter you make a string, the higher the note will be. In a musical bow, bending the two ends away from each other puts more tension on the string, and the pitch of the note gets higher. Bending the two ends closer together reduces the tension, making the string vibrate slower. In guitars and violins, tuning pegs tighten and loosen the strings.

Our Findings

Analysis

1. The sound is produced by the vibrating bowstring.
2. When the ends of the bow are pushed together, the string got looser and the pitch got lower.
3. When the ends of the bow are pulled apart, the string got tighter and the pitch got higher.
4. In stringed instruments, the tighter the string is, the higher the note will be.

PYTHAGORAS AND HIS STRING THEORY

If you have ever looked closely at a guitar or violin, or opened the top of a piano, you probably noticed that the strings are different lengths. The length of the string helps determine the note that the string plays. One of the first people to actually understand the relationship between the length of a vibrating string and its pitch was the Greek mathematician Pythagoras. In **Experiment 13: *Octaves and Intervals***, you will test to see how changing the length of a string affects its pitch. In the process, you will put Pythagoras's string theory to the test.

EXPERIMENT 13: Octaves and Intervals

Topic

How does the length of a vibrating string control the pitch of the note that it produces?

Introduction

There are many mathematical relationships in music, but the Greek philosopher Pythagoras discovered one of the most important more than 2,500 years ago. Born about 580 B.C., Pythagoras made many contributions to mathematics, including his famous theorem about the lengths of the sides of a right triangle. Pythagoras believed that everything in nature had regular patterns that could be described by mathematical relationships, and he spent much of his life trying to work out these relationships.

According to legend, Pythagoras was watching a blacksmith hammering on an anvil. Each time the hammer hit the anvil, it made a ringing sound. When the blacksmith changed the size of the hammer he was using, the sound also changed. This supposedly triggered Pythagoras's search for a mathematical rule to explain the relationship between the pitch of a note and the size of a musical instrument. He began experimenting with strings of different lengths and discovered a fundamental rule that has governed music for more than two thousand years. In this activity, you are going to construct a simple zither that will allow you to put Pythagoras's theory to the test.

Time Required

30 minutes

Materials

- large, flat, wooden board about 24 in. long x 6 in. wide and 1 in. thick (60 cm x 15 cm x 2 cm)
- 2 wood screws, each about 1 ½ in. long
- screwdriver to match the screw heads

- yardstick or meterstick
- pencil
- roll of string
- scissors
- piano or electric keyboard

Safety Note No special safety precautions are needed for this activity. Please review and follow the safety guidelines before proceeding.

Procedure

1. Use the yardstick and pencil to mark two points 16 in. (40 cm) apart on the middle of the wooden board. Place one screw on top of each pencil mark and use the screwdriver to tighten the screws so that about 1 in. (2 cm) of each screw is sticking out of the board.

2. Tie the loose end of the string around one screw. Make sure the knot is tight. This screw will be the binding post. Stretch the string tightly across the board and wrap it around the head of the other screw. Measure about 4 in. (10 cm) of extra string past this screw and cut the string. Tie the loose end of the string around the screw, keeping the string between the screws stretched as tightly as possible. This second screw will be the tuning peg. Your zither is now complete. It should look like Figure 1.

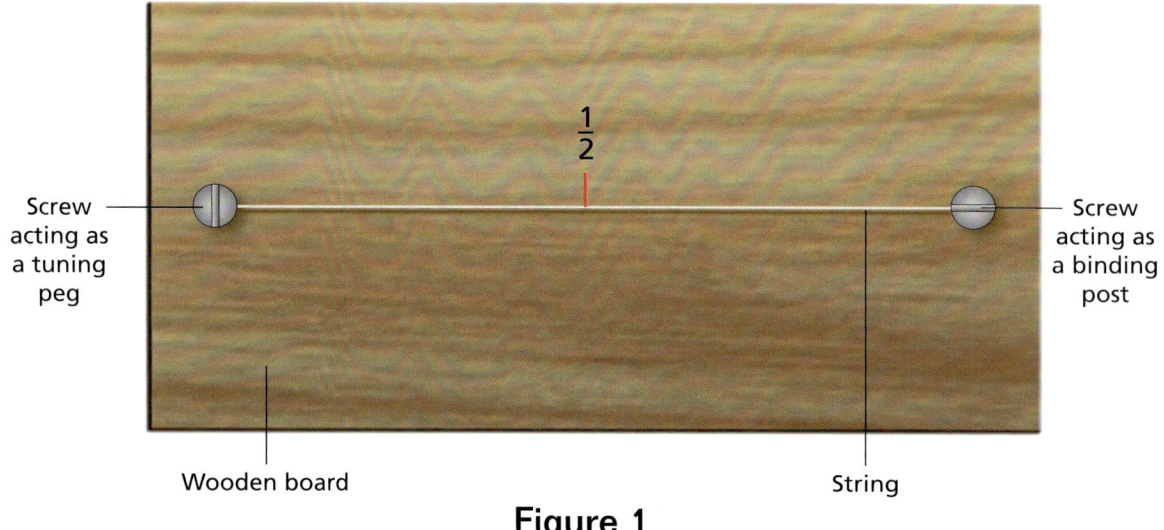

Figure 1

© Infobase Publishing

3. Pluck the string a few times. It should vibrate freely without hitting the board. Slowly turn the tuning peg screw about half a turn clockwise (into the board). Listen to the sound as you pluck the string, and then loosen the screw again. Turn the screw until you get a clear note, and then find that note on the keyboard.

4. Press the pencil on the string about 1 in. (2 cm) from the tuning peg, so that the string is tight against the wooden board. Begin plucking the string and as you do, slowly slide the pencil up the string toward the other screw. Listen carefully to the pitch of the string as you move the pencil.

5. Use the yardstick to measure a point halfway between the two screws and mark it with a pencil. The point should be about 8 in. (20 cm) from the tuning peg. Push down on the pencil at the halfway point so that it is tight against the board. Pluck the string. Listen to the note and find it on the keyboard. Release the string and pluck it again. Find this note on the keyboard.

6. Use the yardstick to measure a point halfway between the center point and the tuning peg. The point should be about 4 in. (10 cm) from the tuning peg. Push the pencil down on the string at this point, pluck the long part of the string, and find the note on the keyboard.

Analysis

1. What happened to the pitch of the string as you slid the pencil from one end of the string to the other?
2. How did the note produced with the full string compare to the note produced with the half-string?
3. How did the note produced with the full string compare with the note produced with the ¾-string?
4. Based on your observations, what is the relationship between the length of a vibrating string and its pitch?

What's Going On?

After conducting many experiments, Pythagoras discovered that vibrating strings with the same tension produce notes of different pitch in exact proportion to their length. For example, if you cut a string in half and don't change the tension on the string, the note it will produce will be eight notes higher, or one "octave" higher, than the note produced by the full string. An octave is an important part of Western music, because it represents the point that a musical note will repeat itself. In other words, if you play a "C" note, the note an octave higher will also be a "C," and so will the note an octave lower.

However, Pythagoras didn't stop at octaves. He also found that if you shortened a string to ⅔ its original length, it would produce a note five notes higher than the original note. A grouping of five notes is also known as a musical "fifth." A string shortened to ¾ its length would produce a note that was four notes higher than the original note. This is called a musical "fourth." These musical intervals represent natural frequencies that are pleasing to the ear. As a result, composers of Western music use these frequencies to create harmonies and blend them to make chords.

Some stringed instruments, such as harps and pianos, have dozens of different strings to produce different notes. Guitars and violins can play the same number of notes using far fewer strings. Different notes are produced by pressing a string against the instrument's neck to shorten its vibrating length. This technique is called stopping, and it's what you did when you held the string against the wooden board with the pencil. Stopping a string at the correct place is much easier when the neck of an instrument has tiny bars built into it that mark the location of specific notes. On a guitar neck, these bars are called frets.

Our Findings

Analysis

1. When you slide the pencil up the string, the pitch of the note gets higher.
2. The note produced with the half-string should be one octave, or eight notes, higher than with the full string.
3. The note produced with the ¾-string should be about four notes higher than the note produced with the full string.
4. As a vibrating string gets shorter, the note it produces has a higher pitch.

SCALING UP: MORE MATHEMATICS IN MUSIC

As previously discussed, mathematics plays a major role in music. Another area in which math is important is the concept of musical scales. In music, the word **scale** usually refers to a gradual progression of notes from one to the next. You are singing a scale when you sing, "Do – re – mi – fa – so – la – ti – do!"

When you pluck a string on a violin, the string will begin vibrating at a certain frequency. This frequency is called the **fundamental**. As we just saw, if you take that same string and divide it in half, it will now play a note that is one octave, or eight notes, higher. If you measured the frequency of the sound waves produced by the half-string, you would find that it was twice the frequency as the full string. In other words, the frequency is doubled when a string is cut in half.

Because of the design of a violin, it is possible to "stop" a string at any point along the neck. This gives the musician an unlimited number of notes. On a piano, however, the number of available frequencies is limited by the keys. If you start at middle "C" on a piano, and move up one note to "D," the frequency of the "D" would be exactly 1.05946 times higher than the frequency of the "C." If you play each key in order, including the black ones, the frequency will increase by 1.05946 times with every key. If you count the number of piano keys in a full octave (both white and black keys), there are not 8 notes, but instead 12 notes, or steps, in the scale. The reason has to do with the mathematical relationship between the frequency of each note and the one before it. Once you reach the first note of the next octave, the frequency has doubled from the first note you played, and the pattern starts again.

MUSICAL NOTES THROUGH THICK AND THIN

So far, we've seen how to change the pitch of a vibrating string by changing either its tension or its length. In addition to testing these relationships, Pythagoras and his followers made another discovery. They found that the thickness of the string also plays a role in producing musical notes. In **Experiment 14:** *Sounds from Vibrating Rubber Bands*, you can discover this relationship by building a simple chordophone using rubber bands.

Experiment 14: Sounds from Vibrating Rubber Bands

Topic

How does the thickness of a vibrating string control the pitch of the note that it produces?

Introduction

If you have ever looked closely at a guitar or inside a piano, you have probably noticed that the strings are not the same thickness. Some are wide; others are thin. As it turns out, the thickness or width of a string plays an important role in controlling the pitch of the note that it produces. In this activity, you will test this relationship by using vibrating rubber bands as models for vibrating strings.

Time Required

30 minutes

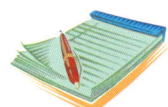

Materials

- lid from a shoebox
- 12-in. (30-cm) ruler
- long pencil
- rubber band "A" – $1/16$ in. (2 mm) thick and $3\frac{1}{2}$ - 4 in. (9-10 cm) long
- rubber band "B" – $1/8$ in. (3 mm) thick and $3\frac{1}{2}$ - 4 in. (9-10 cm) long

Safety Note Please follow the safety guidelines. Be careful not to stretch the rubber bands too far because they can snap.

Procedure

1. Lay the box lid flat on a table with the open side facing up. Stretch the rubber bands around the lid so that they are about 4 in. (10 cm) apart (see Figure 1). Make sure that the rubber bands are stretched evenly all around the lid; if they are tighter in one place than another, your results may not be accurate.

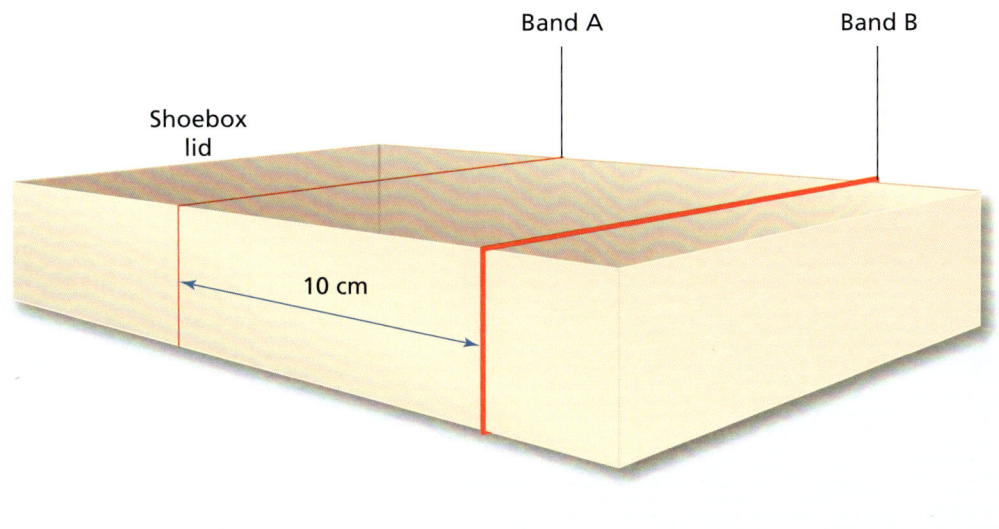

Figure 1

© Infobase Publishing

2. Pluck each rubber band several times to make sure they can vibrate freely. Flip the box lid. Use the ruler to measure 1 ½ in. (4 cm) from the top edge of the box, where each rubber band crosses. Mark each point on the box next to the rubber band with a pencil. Next, measure 3 in. (8 cm) from the top edge of the box and mark these points as well.

3. Insert the pencil under the two rubber bands so that it is resting on the 1 ½ in. (4 cm) marks you just made. After you have inserted the pencil, make sure that the tension on the two rubber bands is even. Pluck the thin rubber band ("band A") several times and listen to the sound it makes. Pluck the thick rubber band ("band B") and listen to the sound it makes. Compare the sounds.

4. Move the pencil down to the 3 in. (8 cm) marks and repeat Step 3.

Analysis

1. Why does the tension in the two rubber bands have to be the same before starting the experiment?
2. Why does the pencil have to be the same distance from the edge of the box for both rubber bands?
3. How did the sound of rubber band A compare with rubber band B at both test locations?
4. Based on your observations, what is the relationship between the thickness of a string and the pitch of the note it produces?

What's Going On?

Back in the sixth century B.C., the Greek mathematician Pythagoras was very interested in the relationship between vibrating strings and the pitch or musical notes they produce. After conducting numerous experiments, he determined that three separate factors control the pitch of a string. First is the tension, or tightness, of the string. The tighter the string is, the higher the note it produces. The second factor is length. The shorter the string is, the higher the note it produces. Third, he discovered that if two strings have equal length and tension, the thinner string produces the higher note.

This third factor has to do with the relative mass of the two strings. If you were to weigh equal lengths of thick string and thin string made from the same material, the thick string always will weigh more. The more mass an object has, the slower it tends to vibrate. The pitch of a note is based on the frequency of vibrations, or how many times a string moves back and forth each second. Because a heavier string vibrates slower than a lighter string, a thicker string will produce a lower note. If you compare the strings on a bass guitar to a regular guitar, you will see that the bass strings are not only longer, but also much thicker. This is why a bass produces lower notes than a regular guitar does.

Our Findings

Analysis

1. Because the tension of the rubber can also affect the pitch, the tension in each band has to be equal in order to test the effect of the thickness.
2. Because the pencil affects the length of the vibrating section of the rubber band, and length affects the pitch, the length of the two rubber bands must be even in order to test the effect of the thickness.
3. Band A should have produced a higher note than band B in both trials.
4. Given two strings of equal length and tension, the thicker string will produce the lower note.

RESONANCE

In the last three experiments, we saw how the pitch of a string varied with its length, tension, and thickness. When a string vibrates, it does so at a certain natural frequency called the **resonant frequency**. This frequency controls the pitch of the note. Strings aren't the only things with resonant frequencies. Drums, pipes, and even bridges and buildings have resonant frequencies. They tend to naturally vibrate at these frequencies. When it comes to the construction of musical instruments, resonant frequencies help to control the quality of the sound. In **Experiment 15:** *Resonance and Musical Instruments*, you will build a simple "resonator" to discover how these natural frequencies can be put to work.

EXPERIMENT 15

Resonance and Musical Instruments

Topic
What is resonance and how does it affect a musical instrument?

Introduction
Somewhere along the way, you may have seen or heard of a demonstration in which a singer hits a certain note and shatters a crystal wine glass. Although it has sometimes been reported as such, the ability of a singer to shatter glass is not a myth. Because sound waves carry energy, they can be used to put things in motion. In some cases, they can have destructive results. The key to breaking a glass with your voice is something called **resonance**. Resonance happens when one vibrating object causes another object to start vibrating. For this to happen, the sound wave must have the same pitch as the resonant frequency of the second object. In this activity, you will put resonance to the test using a coffee can and a keyboard.

Time Required
45 minutes

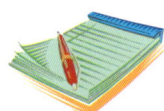

Materials
- piano or electronic keyboard
- small, empty coffee can with lid removed
- 1 12-in. (30-cm) round balloon
- ruler
- 2 large rubber bands
- scissors
- 20 grains of uncooked rice
- roll of masking tape

> **Safety Note** No special safety precautions are needed for this activity. Please review and follow the safety guidelines before proceeding.

Procedure

1. Cut the valve off the balloon. You will be left with a curved sheet of rubber. Stretch the rubber sheet over the open end of the coffee can and wrap the two rubber bands around the top to secure it in place (see Figure 1).

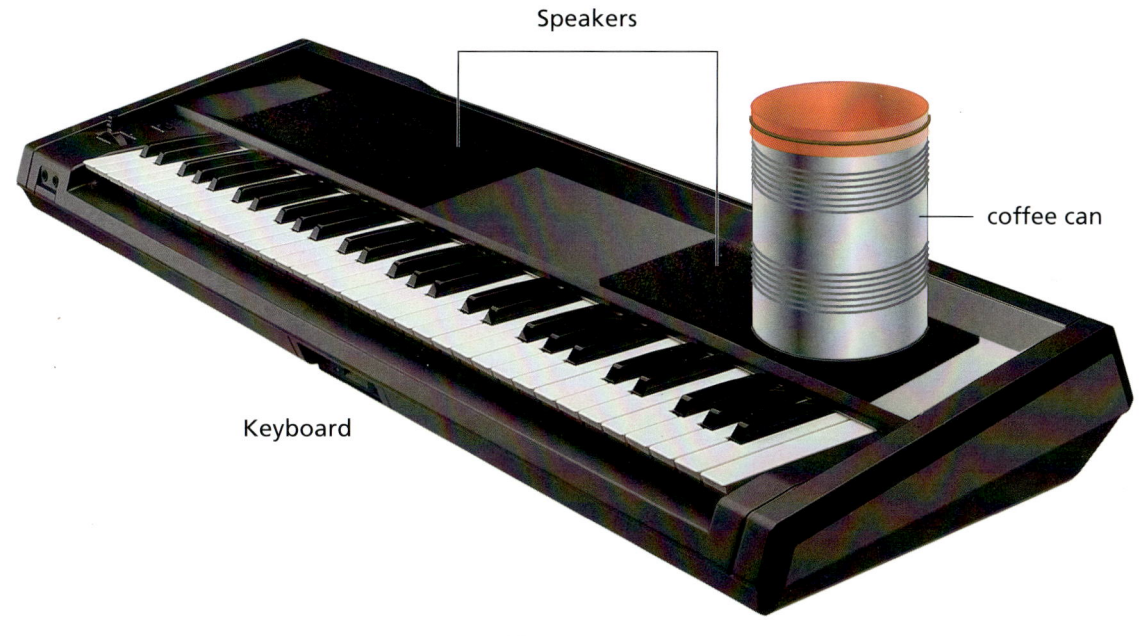

Figure 1

© Infobase Publishing

2. Place the coffee can on top of the speaker of an electronic keyboard. If the keyboard has an instrument selector, set it to "organ." Turn the volume up high. If you are using a standard acoustic piano, place the coffee can on top of the piano and remove the objects from the piano lid.

3. Place about 10 grains of rice on top of the balloon. Play the lowest note on the keyboard (left side). Hold the key down for about 3 seconds and observe the rice on top of the can. If the rice bounces up and down on top of the can, tear off a piece of masking tape and place it on the key you just played.

4. After you have played the first note, repeat Step 3 with each key, placing a piece of tape on any key that makes the rice vibrate. Work your way up the keyboard until you have played 20 notes. Observe what happens to the rice on the coffee can each time a note is played.

5. After you have tested 20 notes, select one of the keys that made the rice vibrate the most. Play that key again and listen carefully to the pitch. Using your voice, try and sing or hum that exact note. After you have practiced a few times, try singing to the coffee can with the rice. Place the coffee can on a table so that it is about 6 in. (15 cm) from your mouth and sing the same note again. Observe what happens to the rice.

Analysis

1. What caused the rice to vibrate on top of the can when the notes were played on the keyboard?
2. Did the rice behave the same time with each note played?
3. How can this experiment help to explain why an opera singer can shatter a wine glass with her voice?

What's Going On?

Resonance is one of the most important properties of any acoustic musical instrument, especially those with strings. Acoustic instruments are not amplified electronically. Resonance makes the instrument sound louder. Resonance also gives the instrument special tonal qualities. When a violin string is played, the string vibrates, which makes a sound. Because the string is small and moves very little air, the sound it produces is soft. The sound that you hear is caused by the body of the violin resonating at the same frequency as the string. Other instruments also resonate, including wind instruments (such as flutes and clarinets), drums, and gongs.

Resonance in musical instruments is a good thing, but resonance in buildings and bridges can cause problems. One of the most famous engineering disasters happened in 1940 at the Tacoma Narrows Bridge in Washington State. Long cables, suspended from towers, held up the main span of the bridge. Just four months after the bridge was completed, the entire bridge deck suddenly began to vibrate wildly in the wind. Within minutes, the entire span collapsed. The bridge didn't collapse because the wind was too strong. The air moving through the cables caused them to vibrate at their resonant frequencies.

Our Findings

Analysis

1. The rice on the can vibrated because the sound wave coming from the keyboard made the coffee can vibrate.
2. The rice did not vibrate the same amount with every note played. Some notes should have produced big vibrations, and others small vibrations. The notes that caused the largest vibrations were those frequencies at which the can naturally vibrated.
3. When an opera singer breaks a glass with her voice, she is singing one of the resonant frequencies of the glass.

PUMPING UP THE VOLUME

Until now, our discussion of chordophones has focused only on how they control the pitch of the notes they produce. Before we move on to the next set of instruments, we will examine how these instruments control their volume. An instrument's volume can be increased either electronically or acoustically. In electronic amplification, the sound waves from the instrument are "picked up" by a microphone or similar device and fed as electronic impulses into a device called an amplifier. This process, which is used at many concerts, has been available for less than 100 years.

When Mozart was writing his symphonies back in the 1700s, electronic amplification wasn't even a dream. Back then, volume was increased acoustically. This usually meant getting an instrument to move more air, creating a sound wave with a larger amplitude. In the last experiment, you saw how tapping into the "natural" or resonant frequencies of a vibrating object could set other objects in motion. In **Experiment 16:** *Amplifying Sound with Resonators*, you will discover how resonance can also be used to amplify the sound coming from a stringed instrument without any help from modern electronics.

EXPERIMENT 16: Amplifying Sound with Resonators

Topic

How do resonators help amplify the volume of a stringed instrument?

Introduction

The maximum volume of a musical instrument is limited by the amount of air that it can cause to vibrate. The more air molecules that are set in motion, the larger the amplitude of a sound wave is, and the louder the sound of the instrument. It can be tricky to design acoustic, or non-amplified, string instruments so they are loud enough to hear. Because a vibrating string touches only a small amount of air, most chordophones solve the problem by using a device called a resonator. In this activity, you are going to construct a simple chordophone and test how different resonators control the volume of the sound that it can produce.

Time Required

45 minutes

Materials

- 4 pieces of kite or package string, each about 2 ft (60 cm) long
- 3 large paper clips
- large (16 oz) disposable plastic cup
- small (8 oz) disposable plastic cup
- large (32 oz) clean deli (salad or soup) container
- electric drill with ¼-in. bit, or an ice pick or similar implement with a point

> **Safety Note** This activity requires adult supervision. Make certain that you and anyone near you are wearing goggles when drilling or punching the holes in the bottom of the plastic containers. Please follow the rest of the safety guidelines.

Procedure

1. Have an adult drill or punch a hole about ¼ in. (5 mm) in diameter into the bottoms of the two plastic cups and the deli container. Do this carefully so the plastic doesn't crack. Once the holes have been made, use your finger to clean off any excess plastic from around the holes.

2. Tie one end of a piece of string to a paper clip. Thread one piece of string through the hole in the small plastic cup, from the inside to the outside. Pull the string all the way through, so the paper clip rests on the bottom of the cup. It should look like Figure 1. Follow the same procedure for the large cup and the deli container. When you are done, you should have three chordophones, each with its own resonator.

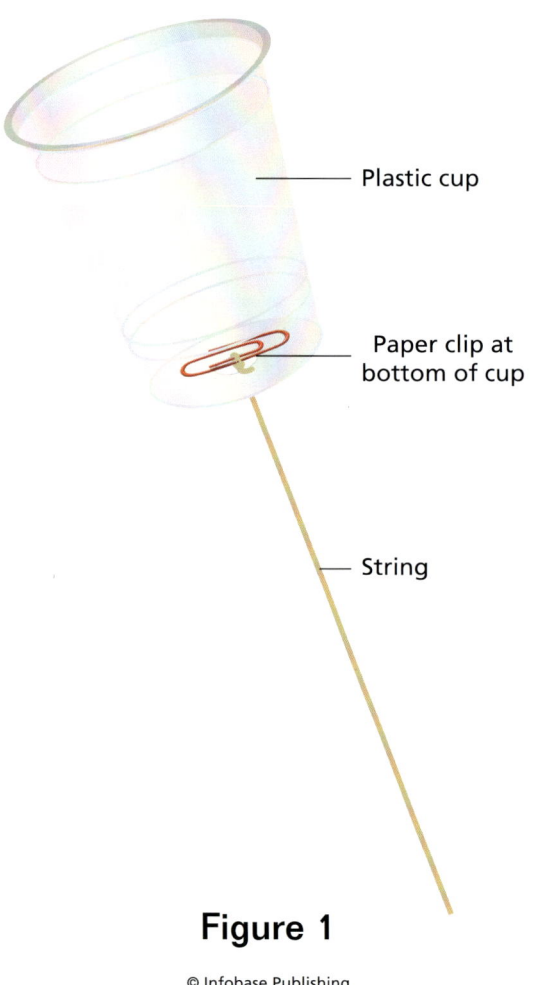

Figure 1

© Infobase Publishing

3. Hold one end of the remaining piece of string in each hand. Pull the string tight. Using one of your thumbs, pluck the string several times. Listen to the sound that the string makes when it begins vibrating.

4. Put the string down and pick up the string with the small cup attached. Hold the cup in one hand and gently pull the string with your other hand until the paper clip is tight against the bottom of the cup. Don't pull too tight; you don't want to crack the cup and pull the paper clip through the hole. Once the string is tight, use your thumb to pluck it several times and listen to the sound it makes. Compare this sound to the sound of the string alone.

5. Put the small cup down and repeat Step 4 with the large cup and the deli container. Compare the sounds that the different strings make.

Analysis

1. How did the volume of the sound of the plain string compare with the volume of the string attached to the small cup?
2. Which of the four strings was loudest when it was plucked?
3. Based on your experiment, what factor do you think was responsible for you getting the results that you did?
4. Based on your experiment, why do you think that a cello normally produces a louder sound than a violin when they are both played the same way?

What's Going On?

By itself, a vibrating string is not a practical instrument because it can move only a small amount of air. Over the years, instrument makers have discovered that to make the sound louder, the string had to be attached to a device called a resonator, or "sound board." In this activity, the three plastic containers acted like resonators. A resonator is simply a large, hard, flexible surface that is in contact with, or "coupled" to, the string. When the string begins vibrating, the vibrations pass into the resonator, and it begins to vibrate at the same frequency (or pitch) as the string. Some resonators, such as the soundboard inside a piano, have large surface areas. This means that once they start vibrating, they move a large volume of air, which amplifies the sound.

In instruments such as acoustic guitars, violins, and cellos, the body of the instrument itself serves as the resonator. The strings of the instrument are coupled to the top of the instrument by a device called a bridge. This is the little piece that holds the strings above the body of the instrument. When the strings vibrate, the bridge allows the vibrations to pass into the top board of the instrument, causing the air inside to vibrate. The vibrating air then escapes from the instrument through holes. In general, the larger the air space inside the instrument, the louder the instrument.

Our Findings

Analysis

1. The plain string was quieter than the string that was attached to the cup.
2. The string that was attached to the deli container made the loudest and deepest sound.
3. The biggest container produced the loudest sound because it held the most air.
4. A cello usually will sound louder than a violin, because it is a larger instrument with more air inside.

SWEET AND SOUR NOTES: THE TONE QUALITY OF STRINGED INSTRUMENTS

If you have ever listened to a symphony orchestra, or to a few people strumming acoustic guitars, you may have noticed that each instrument sounds just a little bit different. A large part of the difference has to do with the talent levels of the people playing the instruments, but several other factors come into play. As we just saw in the last experiment, the sounds that come from an instrument are not just the result of vibrating strings. The design of the instrument body plays an important role, too. Two instruments can appear identical, but there's a good chance that they won't sound the same. Small variations in wood thickness, wood density, and even the amount and type of glue used in construction will affect an instrument's resonant frequencies.

Musicians usually refer to these differences in sound as the timbre. This is nothing more than the quality of the sound. As it turns out, when a musician plays a note on an instrument, the fundamental frequency isn't the only sound you hear. Depending on the type of instrument, a number of **harmonics**, or overtones, are produced. These other frequencies are difficult to detect, but they give an instrument its timbre, or particular sound quality. In fact, among violins, differences in sound quality can mean the difference between an instrument that costs several hundred dollars and one that costs several million.

Next, we are going to explore some of the science behind **aerophones**, or wind instruments. Many of the same principles involving pitch, resonance, and timbre hold true for aerophones, too. The names of the instruments may have changed, but the ideas are very much the same.

4

The Wind Instruments

Aerophones, or wind instruments, date back many thousands of years. We may never know who first came up with the idea of blowing into a hollow reed or a seashell to make a sound, but those early musical innovators opened the door to a variety of instruments, ranging from flutes and saxophones to bagpipes and tubas.

An aerophone is a musical instrument that produces sound by means of a vibrating column of air. Most often, a person blows into the instrument to set the air in motion, but this is not always the case. Accordions and pipe organs are aerophones that get their air from a pump, bellows, or a mechanical blower.

Aerophones fall into categories based on the way the vibration is made. Members of the flute family have some type of blowhole that channels the air into the instrument. True flutes include side-blown instruments, which are commonly found in bands and orchestras today, as well as more traditional end-blown instruments, such as the one you made in **Experiment 10**: *Effect of Tube Length on Sound Pitch*. Related to the flutes are aerophones that have a whistle mouthpiece, such as recorders or song flutes. In both of these groups, the air vibrates when it strikes a sharp edge at the front end the instrument.

The reed family includes instruments such as saxophones, clarinets, oboes, and bagpipes. As the name suggests, all of these instruments get air vibrating by means of either a single or double reed, often set into a mouthpiece. Harmonicas and accordions also use reeds to get the air vibrating, but neither

A clarinet (*left*) is an aerophone that belongs to the reed family. A reed in the mouthpiece (*right*) causes the air to vibrate, thereby producing sound.

has a mouthpiece. Reed instruments are very different from instruments in the horn family, which usually have cup-shaped mouthpieces. In a horn, such as a trumpet or trombone, the musician has to make his or her lips vibrate to start the air vibrating in the instrument. Regardless of how they get the air vibrating, aerophones are some of the most popular instruments of beginning band students around the world.

CONTROLLING THE FLOW

As you discovered in **Experiment 10:** *Effect of Tube Length on Sound Pitch*, one way of controlling the pitch of an aerophone is by controlling the length of the vibrating air column inside it. To play different notes on panpipes, you have to blow into different-sized tubes. This means you have to keep moving the instrument back and forth, directing the air into different tubes. As it turns out, a single tube can be modified in two ways to produce a wide range of notes. In **Experiment 17:** *Controlling the Pitch of Recorders and Song Flutes*, you will discover how a few well-placed holes can liven up a tune.

EXPERIMENT 17: Controlling the Pitch of Recorders and Song Flutes

Topic

How do the holes in a wind instrument help control the pitch?

Introduction

One of the most common wind instruments played in schools today is the recorder. A recorder is a type of "whistle flute" that was first developed back in the 1300s. Like most aerophones or wind instruments, a recorder produces a musical note by getting a column of air inside of it to vibrate. Unlike a modern concert flute, which has a simple blowhole, a recorder has a mouth-

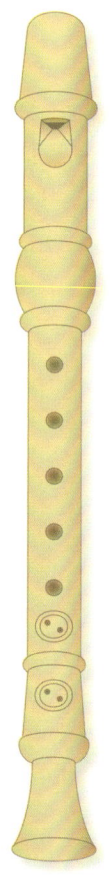

Figure 1

© Infobase Publishing

piece that resembles a whistle. When air is blown into the mouthpiece, it is deflected against a sharp edge of a hole that has been cut into the pipe. This movement gets the air vibrating, which produces a sound. A series of holes along the body of the instrument allow a musician to change the pitch of the note that the recorder plays. In this activity, you will examine the placement of the holes to determine how they control the pitch of the instrument.

Time Required

30 minutes

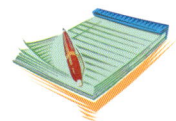

Materials

- recorder (or Flutophone) with removable mouthpiece
- 1-liter soda bottle, half-filled with water

Safety Note No special safety precautions are needed for this activity. Please review and follow the safety guidelines before proceeding.

Procedure

1. Blow across the top of the water-filled bottle. Listen to the sound. Pour about half of the water out of the bottle and blow across the top again. Compare the sound with the first sound. Pour all of the water out of the bottle and then blow across the top a third time. Compare this sound with the first two sounds.

2. Remove the mouthpiece from the recorder and blow through it several times. Do not cover the bottom end with your hand. Listen to the sound that it makes.

3. Blow through the mouthpiece again. Put the mouthpiece back on the recorder. Blow through the recorder with the mouthpiece on, making sure not to cover any of the holes. Compare the sound of the mouthpiece alone to the sound of the recorder with all holes open.

4. Look closely at the recorder. Along the top should be a series of seven holes for your fingers. Turn the recorder over and look at the underside, opposite the finger holes. There should be a single hole for your thumb. Blow into the recorder with an easy, steady stream of air. While you do

this, cover and uncover the thumbhole. Do not cover any of the other holes. Compare the sounds that the recorder makes when the thumbhole is open and closed.

5. Blow into the recorder with an easy, steady stream of air with all the holes open. Continue to blow, and cover the thumbhole, the finger hole closest to the mouthpiece, the second finger hole, and the third finger hole. Listen to the sound of the recorder as you cover each hole and compare the pitch each time you close a hole.

Analysis

1. What happened to the pitch of the sound that the bottle produced as you kept emptying water from the bottle?
2. How did the sound of the mouthpiece alone compare to the sound of the entire recorder with all the holes open?
3. How did the sound of the recorder with all the holes open compare to the sound of the recorder with the thumbhole covered?
4. What happened to the pitch of the recorder as you blew through it and covered the holes along the body of the instrument?
5. Based on your experiment, how are the finger holes on the recorder similar to the bottle filled with different amounts of water?

What's Going On?

When you blow across the top of a bottle, or into an aerophone such as a recorder or flute, the sound is produced by the vibrating column of air inside. As the air begins to vibrate, it creates a standing wave, with a wavelength controlled by the length of the air column. Longer air columns produce standing waves with longer wavelengths. With sound waves, there is a direct relationship between the wavelength and frequency, or the number of times the wave vibrates per second. The longer the wavelength is, the lower the frequency of vibrations. Frequency controls the pitch of the sound. The lower the frequency, the lower or deeper the note is.

When you blow into the bottle, the length of the air column is controlled by how much water there is. If there is more water, the air column is shorter and the note is higher in pitch. The recorder works the same way, but it has holes that allow the player to lengthen or shorten the vibrating air column.

When you played only the mouthpiece, the air column is very short. The sound produced is very high pitched. When the body of the recorder is attached to the mouthpiece, the air column gets longer and the note's pitch gets lower. Some of the air is coming out of the other holes, as well. The thumbhole is closest to the mouthpiece, so it has the most control over the length of the standing wave inside the instrument.

Covering the thumbhole forces more air to come out the first finger hole on top of the instrument, which is farther down the tube than the thumbhole. This action makes the vibrating air column longer, so it makes a lower note. Covering each successive hole on the recorder lengthens the vibrating air column. This increases the length of the standing wave and decreases the frequency of the vibrations, so the note keeps getting lower. You may have found that sometimes you got a high-pitched squeal coming out of the recorder. This usually happens when you blow too hard. You are forcing too much air into the instrument, so some of the air comes back out through the mouthpiece. The mouthpiece has a very short standing wave, so it makes a high-pitched sound. To play an aerophone correctly, you need a gentle, steady stream of air moving through the body of the instrument.

Our Findings

Analysis

1. As you decreased the amount of water in the bottle, the pitch of the note got lower.
2. Blowing in the assembled recorder produced a lower note than blowing through the mouthpiece alone.
3. Covering the thumbhole of the recorder produced a lower note than leaving the thumbhole open.
4. As you cover more finger holes, the pitch of the recorder gets lower.
5. The more air in the bottle, the lower the note. The longer the column of air in the recorder, the lower the note.

THE LONG AND THE SHORT OF IT

In the previous experiment, we saw how opening and closing different holes in the body of a recorder allows a musician to control the pitch of the note that's played. This same process also works for most other members of the woodwind family, including clarinets, saxophones, and bassoons. For brass instruments, such as trumpets, the process is a little different. Instead of opening and closing holes, these aerophones are controlled by valves. In **Experiment 18:** *Creating Sounds with a Trombone*, you will experiment with building a simple slide valve to change the length of a vibrating air tube.

EXPERIMENT 18
Creating Sounds with a Trombone

Topic
How does the slide valve on a trombone help control the pitch of the note?

Introduction
Trombones, trumpets, bugles, and tubas are wind instruments called aerophones. They all are members of the horn family. Each has a cup-shaped mouthpiece through which the musician blows. In a simple horn, such as a bugle, the musician changes the pitch of the note by changing the way he or she blows into it. In trumpets and tubas, the positions of the mouth and lips also are used to change the note, but these instruments also have valves to control the flow of air. The trombone is unique. It uses a slide valve to control the flow of air. In this activity, you are going to construct a simple pitch pipe with a slide valve and test to see how it controls the pitch of a note.

Time Required
30 minutes

Materials
- 2 plastic drinking straws of equal length but with different diameters. Each should be at least ³⁄₈ in. or 1 cm wide. (Fast food restaurants and convenience stores that sell large fountain drinks are good sources for extra-wide drinking straws.)
- small ball of modeling clay
- roll of cellophane tape
- ruler
- scissors

> **Safety Note** No special safety precautions are needed for this activity. Please review and follow the safety guidelines before proceeding.

Procedure

1. Lay the two straws next to each other. If one straw is longer than the other, use the scissors to trim it so that it is the same length as the shorter straw.
2. Hold the wider straw up to your lower lip and blow across the top so that you produce a sound. Do the same thing with the thinner straw. Compare the pitches of the sounds.
3. Repeat Step 2, but hold a finger over the bottom of the straw so that the end is sealed. Compare the sounds of the sealed straws with the sounds of the open-ended straws.
4. Take the end of the thinner straw and slide it into the thicker straw. It should fit snugly but still be able to slide in and out. If the thinner straw is too loose, wrap a small piece of cellophane tape around the end to make it fit snugly. Do not seal the bottom hole in the straw with the tape.

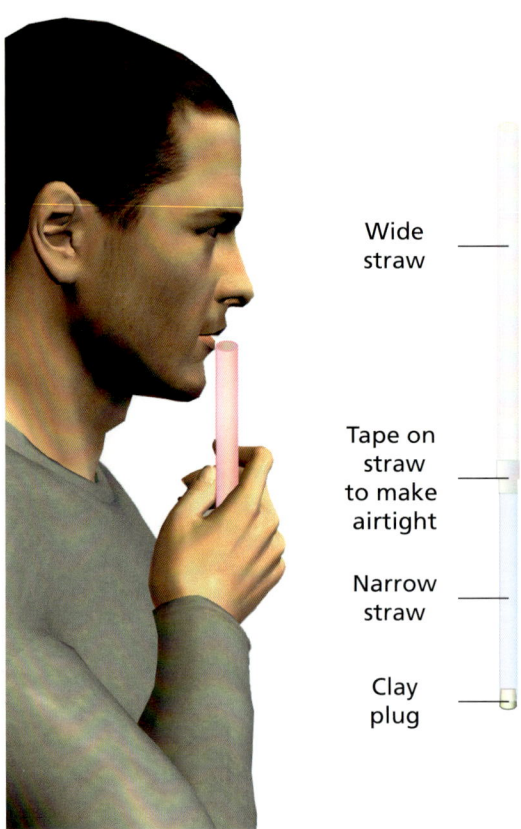

Figure 1

© Infobase Publishing

5. After you have connected the two straws, take a small piece of clay and plug the end of the thinner straw. Push the taped end of the thinner straw into the thicker straw until only about 1 in. (2 cm) sticks out. Blow across the top of the thicker straw and compare the sound it makes to the sound the straws made in Step 2. As you are blowing, slowly pull the thinner straw out of the thicker straw. Do not pull it out all the way. Listen to the sound of the straw as you pull it out, and then keep blowing as you push it in again. Listen to what happens to the sound of the straw as you move it in and out while blowing across the open end.

Analysis

1. How did the pitch of the two straws sound when you blew across them separately?
2. What happened to the pitch of the straws when you blocked the lower end?
3. Why is it important that the seal between the two straws be tight?
4. What happened to the pitch of the note as you pulled the thinner straw in and out of the thicker straw?

What's Going On?

In wind instruments, one way to change the pitch of a note is to change the length of the vibrating air column inside. A trumpet or tuba has valves that change the direction of airflow inside the instrument. Pressing a valve sends the air to a longer or shorter tube, changing the length of the vibrating air column. In a trombone, the valve system is much simpler. The slide of the instrument is one long valve. It is made from a U-shaped piece of tubing that connects to another tube. When the slide is pulled out, the air column is made longer. This causes the air inside the instrument to vibrate at a lower frequency, which lowers the pitch of the note. Pushing the slide back into the instrument has the opposite effect. It shortens the air column and increases the frequency of the vibrations, creating a note with a higher pitch. The simple slide whistle that you made using the straws works the same way as the trombone slide does. By moving the slide valve back and forth, a trombone player can play many notes and get a workout, too.

Our Findings

Analysis

1. Though they had different diameters, both straws should have produced the same note.

2. Blocking the end of each straw made it produce a note with a lower pitch.
3. The two straws had to fit snugly together so that no air would leak out.
4. As you pull the thinner straw out, the pitch gets lower. When you push it back in, the pitch gets higher.

RESONANCE IN WIND INSTRUMENTS

Previously, we looked at how resonance not only gave chordophones their unique sound quality, but also played an important role in making them louder. As you might have guessed, resonance also comes into play in many wind instruments. As a column of air vibrates inside an aerophone, it also causes the body of the instrument to resonate. In fact, without resonance, the sound generated from a vibrating reed or a pair of lips would be almost too quiet to hear. One of the best ways to see how resonance works in a wind instrument is to build and play a horn called a didgeridoo. In **Experiment 19: Making a Didgeridoo to Test Resonance**, you will discover how a hollow tube can turn a pair of vibrating lips into a marvelous musical instrument.

To create sound with a didgeridoo, a person needs to vibrate his or her lips when blowing air into the instrument. The vibrations caused by the person's lips create waves, and the closer those waves are to the natural resonant frequency of the didgeridoo, the stronger the air will vibrate in the instrument. The instrument will amplify the waves and the sound will then be louder than the sound produced by the lips alone.

Making a Didgeridoo to Test Resonance

Topic

How can resonance make the sound produced by vibrating lips louder?

Introduction

One of the simplest wind instruments comes from Australia. Called a didgeridoo (pronounced **DID- jer- ree- doo**), it looks like a long, hollow branch. According to historians, aboriginal Australians have used didgeridoos for more than 1,500 years. They are still used today in special ceremonies. Most traditional didgeridoos are made of wood or bamboo. Often, they are made from the trunk or large branches of a eucalyptus tree that has been naturally hollowed out by termites. A didgeridoo is about 5 ft (1 ½ m) long. At one end, it has a ring of wax for a mouthpiece. In this activity, you will construct a didgeridoo from a piece of PVC pipe and use it to examine how resonance works in wind instruments.

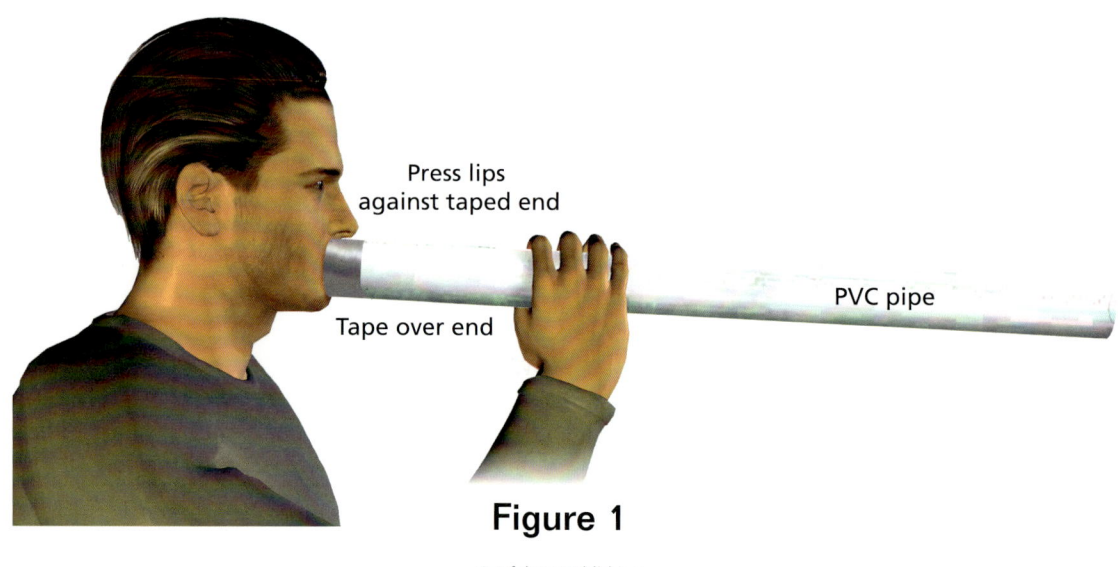

Figure 1

© Infobase Publishing

Time Required

30 minutes

 **Materials**

- piece of PVC pipe about 5 ft (1 ½ m) long. The pipe should have a diameter of about 1 ½ in. (4 cm). (This is a standard size that is available in most home improvement or plumbing supply stores.)
- roll of duct tape
- ruler
- scissors

Safety Note No special safety precautions are needed for this activity. If the pipe has to be cut, ask an adult to help you. Please review and follow the safety guidelines before proceeding.

Procedure

1. Cut a piece of duct tape about 8 in. (20 cm) long. Wrap the duct tape around one end of the PVC pipe so that it overlaps the edge by about ½ in. (1 cm). Fold the overlap of duct tape into the pipe to make the mouthpiece.
2. Before you can play the didgeridoo, you will have to practice vibrating your lips. Begin by slowly blowing through your closed lips so that they flap and buzz, making a sound like a motorboat. Then try blowing a little harder, so that your lips begin vibrating faster. Compare the sounds of your lips vibrating fast and vibrating slowly.
3. Hold the duct-taped end of the pipe to your mouth. Try blowing into the pipe without vibrating your lips, and listen to the sound.
4. Repeat Step 3, but vibrate your lips slowly when you blow into the pipe. Compare the sound coming out of the pipe with the sound of your lips alone. When you blow, try to keep the air stream steady and don't blow too hard.
5. After you get comfortable blowing into the pipe, try vibrating your lips at different speeds and see how many sounds you can get out of your didgeridoo!

Analysis

1. How did the sound of your lips vibrating slowly compare to the sound of your lips when they were vibrating fast?

2. What sound came out of the pipe when you blew into it without vibrating your lips?

3. How did the sound of your lips vibrating alone compare to the sound that your vibrating lips made when you played the didgeridoo?

What's Going On?

Even though it doesn't look like it, the didgeridoo is a trumpet. Trumpets, trombones, tubas, and didgeridoos all belong to the same group of aerophones (wind instruments). They each have a cup-shaped mouthpiece. In order to produce a sound, a trumpet player must first begin vibrating his or her lips. This vibrates the air inside the instrument, which produces the musical notes. By tightening the opening between your lips and blowing harder or softer, you can get your lips to produce different notes. The faster your lips vibrate, the higher the pitch of the note produced.

When vibrating air enters a didgeridoo or a modern trumpet, it produces sound waves of different lengths and frequencies inside the instrument. These waves will interfere with each other, and some will get cancelled out. Those waves that come close to matching the natural resonant frequency of the instrument will cause the air in the instrument to vibrate the strongest. As a result, they are amplified by the instrument itself. The sound that comes out of the instrument for those particular notes is much louder than the sound produced by the lips alone. An experienced didgeridoo player can match the vibrations of his or her lips to the resonant frequencies of the tube. When this happens, the instrument will produce a moaning sound called a drone.

Our Findings

Analysis

1. The faster your lips move, the higher the pitch of the sound produced.
2. When you blow into the pipe without vibrating your lips, hardly any sound is made.
3. When you blow into the didgeridoo with your lips vibrating slowly, the sound that comes out is lower, louder, and deeper than the sound made with the lips alone.

AMPLIFYING AEROPHONES

In the previous experiment, we saw how the vibrating air column inside the body of an aerophone helps to amplify the sound of the instrument. This is similar to the way that the air inside the hollow body of a violin helps to make it louder. Most wind instruments tend to be louder than stringed instruments. Part of the difference in volume is due to the way an aerophone is played. When a musician blows into a wind instrument, he or she is forcing extra air inside, which increases the amplitude of the sound wave that is produced. There is another reason for the louder sound of a wind instrument. In **Experiment 20: *How a Wind Instrument's Shape Affects its Sound*,** you will test to see how the shape of a wind instrument helps to amplify its sound.

EXPERIMENT 20: How a Wind Instrument's Shape Affects its Sound

Topic

How does the shape of a wind instrument affect the volume of the sound that it produces?

Introduction

If you have ever taken a close look at the design of a trumpet, tuba, or saxophone, you've probably noticed that each one ends in a flared or funnel-shaped opening called a bell. The bell isn't there to make the instrument look good. There is a practical reason that designers use this shape in constructing these instruments. In this activity, you will construct two horns with different shapes to find out which has a greater effect on the volume of a wind instrument.

Time Required

30 minutes

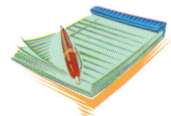

Materials

- personal music player (iPod or other mp3 player, or portable CD player) with ear bud headphones
- 2 pieces of 8 ½-in. x 11-in. standard-sized copier (or other thin) paper
- scissors
- ruler with inches
- cellophane tape

Safety Note No special safety precautions are needed for this activity. Please review and follow the safety guidelines before proceeding.

Procedure

1. Roll one piece of paper into a cylinder with a diameter of about 1 in. (2 cm). The tube should be 8 ½ in. (21 cm) long. Use the tape to keep the cylinder from unrolling. Fold and roll the second piece of paper into a cone according to the pattern in Figure 1. The small opening of the cone should also be about 1 in. (2 cm) in diameter and the large end of the cone should be about 3 in. (8 cm) across.

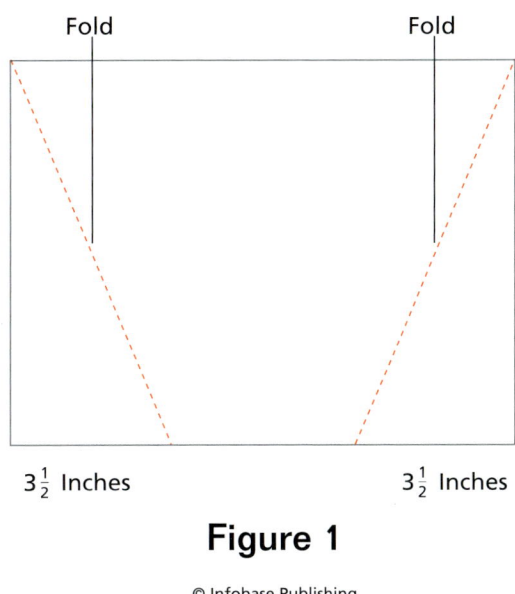

Figure 1

© Infobase Publishing

2. Plug the ear buds into your personal music player and turn the volume up as high as it will go. Start playing a piece of music with a fairly constant sound level. Hold one of the ear buds about 2 ft (60 cm) in front of you. **Do not put the ear bud in your ear**. Listen to the volume of the music coming from the ear bud.

3. Place the ear bud into the bottom of the paper cylinder and hold it so that the front end of the cylinder is about 2 ft (60 cm) in front of you. Point the cylinder at your face. Turn the cylinder from side to side and listen to the sound. Compare the sound of the music when it is coming through the cylinder to when it is coming out of the ear bud alone. Compare the sound coming from the cylinder when it is pointed straight at you to when it is pointed to either side.

4. Repeat Step 3 with the paper cone (see Figure 2). Place the ear bud into the narrow end of the cone. Hold the cone the same distance from your face as you held the cylinder. Compare the sound of the music coming through the cone to the sound that came through the cylinder and the ear bud alone.

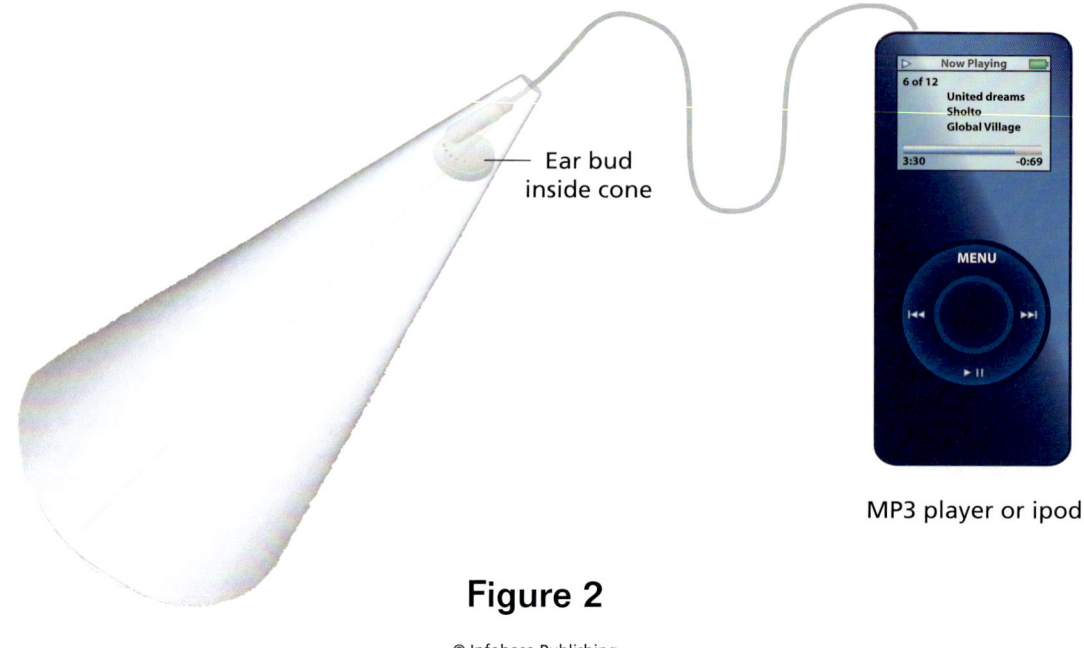

Figure 2

© Infobase Publishing

Analysis

1. How did the sound of the music coming out of the ear bud alone compare to the sound coming through the paper cylinder?
2. What happened to the sound of the music coming through the cylinder when you turned it from side to side?
3. How did the sound of the music coming through the cone compare to the sound that came through the cylinder?
4. Based on this experiment, why do you think that a wind instrument often has a flared opening at its lower end?

What's Going On?

When sound comes out of a small speaker, such as an ear bud, the sound waves travel in all directions and quickly run out of energy. Unless the speaker is very close to (or in) your ear, the sound is quite soft. Placing the ear bud into the bottom of a cylinder traps the sounds waves in the cylinder. This gets the air inside the cylinder moving. Because more sound waves are moving along the same pathway, the sound coming out of the cylinder is louder than with the ear bud alone. You get the same effect if you cup your hands around your mouth when you shout across an open field. The problem is that you have to be in a direct line with the tube in order to hear the amplified sound. If you are off to either side, the sound is actually quieter than with the ear bud alone, because most of the sound waves pass by you.

When you put the ear bud in the paper cone, the sound becomes louder. Like the cylinder, the cone is trapping the sound waves and sending them in the same general direction. Unlike the cylinder, the end of the cone is flared. This projects the sound waves over a wider area. You don't have to be directly in front of the cone to hear the amplified sound. If you are standing off to the side, many of the sound waves can still reach you. The flared end or bell of a wind instrument works like a megaphone.

Our Findings

Analysis

1. The music coming through the paper cylinder was a little louder and had a deeper tone than the ear bud alone.
2. The music coming through the paper cylinder was loudest when it was pointed straight at you. When it was pointed to the sides, the sound was quieter.
3. The music coming through the paper cone was louder than with the cylinder. When the cone was turned in different directions, the sound level was reduced a little, but not as much as with the cylinder.
4. The flared end of a wind instrument increases the volume of the instrument and helps to project the sound to the audience.

TONE QUALITY IN AEROPHONES: WOOD VS. METAL

In Unit 3, we discussed how the design and construction of a chordophone affects the way that it resonates. This, in turn, has a major impact on the overall sound quality of the instrument. In aerophones, the same general rules apply. In addition to body size and shape, an instrument's material also controls its tone. Most stringed instruments are made from wood, but aerophones can be made from wood, metal, plastic, or even bone and stone. In fact, wind instruments were originally placed into different groups depending on the material from which they were made. As you might have guessed, members of the brass family, such as trumpets and trombones, are made of brass. Woodwind instruments—including clarinets, saxophones, and flutes—all were originally made from wood, but now can be made from brass, silver, and even plastic. In **Experiment 21: *Vibrations Through Various Materials***, you will see how different materials can affect the sound quality of the same musical note.

EXPERIMENT 21
Vibrations Through Various Materials

Topic
How does the material from which it is made affect the sound quality of a musical instrument?

Introduction
If a vibrating object is placed near or against a motionless object, the second object often will begin vibrating. This is an example of what scientists call **forced vibrations**. Some of the mechanical energy in the vibrating object is transferred to the second object, setting it in motion. Forced vibrations are important in many musical instruments, because they help to amplify sound. Yet, not all materials vibrate the same way. In this activity, you will use a tuning fork to create forced vibrations in three materials to determine the effects on sound quality.

Time Required
30 minutes

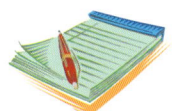

Materials
- tuning fork
- wooden spoon or drumstick
- 2 thick rubber bands
- 2 large books about the same size and thickness
- metal baking pan (9 in. x 13 in. [23 cm x 32 cm]) or large metal mixing bowl
- wooden board, about 9 in. long x 12 in. wide x 1 in. thick (23 cm x 30 cm x 2 cm)

- sheet of thick, hard plastic (a plastic cutting board or a lunch tray works well)
- ruler

Safety Note No special safety precautions are needed for this activity. Please review and follow the safety guidelines before proceeding.

Procedure

1. Place the two books about 8 in. (20 cm) apart on a table or other flat surface. Place the wooden board on top of the books so that it acts as a bridge. The set-up should look like Figure 1.

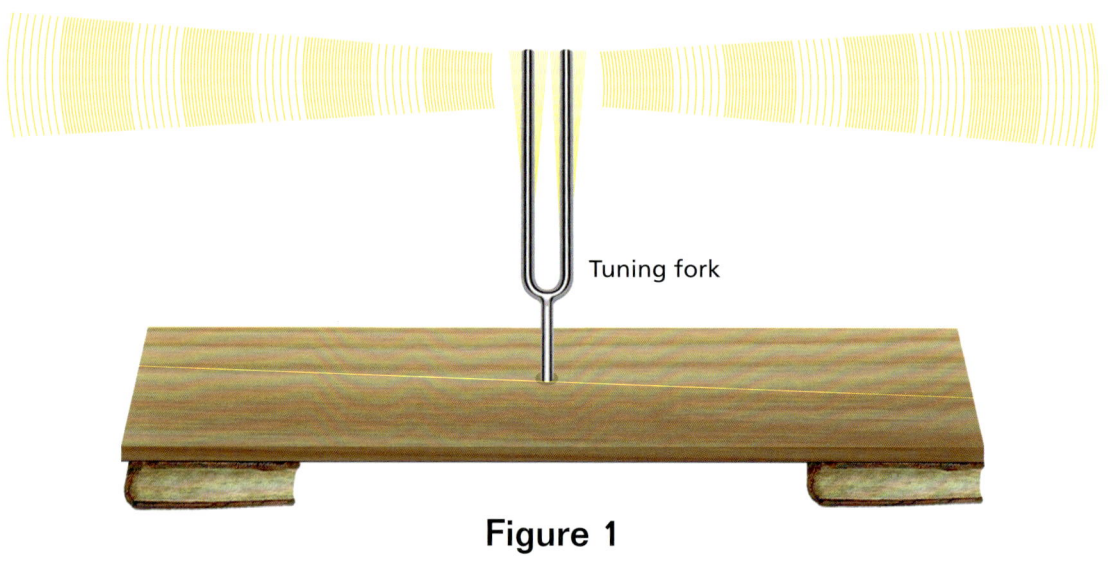

Figure 1

© Infobase Publishing

2. Wrap several rubber bands around the end of the wooden spoon or drumstick. This is the mallet for striking the tuning fork. (Never hit a tuning fork against a hard object; this could crack it.) Hold the tuning fork by the handle and strike the tines with the rubber end of the stick. Listen to the sound. Strike the tuning fork again, and while it is still vibrating, touch the bottom of the fork against the top of the wooden board. Compare this sound to the sound of the tuning fork alone.

3. Remove the wooden board and place the plastic sheet on top of the two books. Repeat Step 2, touching the vibrating tuning fork to the plastic. Compare the sound to the sound made with the wooden board.

4. Remove the plastic sheet and place the metal pan or mixing bowl upside-down on top of the books. Repeat Step 2. Compare the sound with the sounds made by the wood and plastic.

Analysis

1. How did the sound of the tuning fork alone compare to the sound of the fork when it was touching the wooden board?
2. How did the sound of the vibrating plastic compare to the vibrating wood?
3. How did the sound of the vibrating metal compare to the sounds of the wood and plastic?
4. What happened to the pitch of note during each trial?

What's Going On?

All objects vibrate at certain natural, or resonant, frequencies. People who make musical instruments take advantage of this fact to amplify sound. When a musician blows into a wind instrument, for example, the vibrations of the reed or lips forces the body of the instrument to vibrate. This causes the air trapped inside the instrument to resonate at the same frequencies, creating a louder sound. The sound quality, or tone, produced by wind instruments will vary with the materials from which they are made. A plastic recorder will sound different from a wooden one, even when the same notes are played. That's because plastic has different resonant frequencies than wood does. This difference is sound quality is called the timbre of an instrument. When an instrument vibrates, it doesn't just produce one note. The resonance also creates a number of harmonics, or overtones, which give the instrument a unique sound quality.

In an orchestra, the brass instruments tend to have a brighter, harsher sound than the woodwinds. Brass is made of copper and zinc. It is relatively hard and dense. When brass vibrates, it tends to resonate with higher-frequency sounds than wood does. Woodwinds tend to produce a more mellow sound because wood is much less dense than brass, and usually softer. Therefore, wooden instruments tend to resonate with lower-frequency sounds.

Our Findings

Analysis

1. The sound of the tuning fork alone is much quieter than when the vibrating fork touches the wood.
2. The vibrating plastic has a different sound than the wood, but the pitch is the same.
3. The metal produces a different sound than either the wood or the plastic. It is much more "tinny," while the sound made by the wood is deeper.
4. The pitch of the note for each trial is the same because the same tuning fork is used for each trial.

FREE AEROPHONES: HEAR THE ROARING BULL

All of the aerophones discussed so far work the same basic way. Each produces musical notes by vibrating a column of air inside the instrument. Not every wind instrument works this way, however. In Unit 1, there was an experiment with a free aerophone. The rope that you spun around in **Experiment 6: How Speed of Vibrations Affects Pitch of Sound** is different from other aerophones. Instead of having air vibrating inside it, this instrument vibrates the air around it.

This type of free aerophone is called a bull-roarer. These instruments date back more than 25,000 years, and they are still used in ceremonial rituals today by many native peoples in Africa, South America, and Asia. The earliest bull-roarer designs used a thin, flat disc of bone or wood tied to the end of some type of cord. To play it, the musician holds onto the free end of the cord and whirls the disc around his head. The moving disc vibrates the air, producing a musical note. The pitch of the note can be changed by whirling the cord faster or slower.

5

Percussion Instruments

Let's explore two groups of related instruments: the **idiophones** and the **membranophones**. Most of the instruments in these groups are percussive, which means they are the heavy hitters of the musical world: bells, gongs, and drums. They usually are played by being hit, rubbed, or shaken.

Idiophones make up the largest and most varied family of musical instruments found around the world today. The word comes from two Greek words: *idios*, which means "self," and *phone*, which means "sound." An idiophone makes sound when the body of the instrument vibrates. Idiophones don't need to have air forced through them like aerophones do. Unlike chordophones, idiophones have no strings attached.

Idiophones can be simple or complex. A stamping stick, which is nothing more than a piece of wood pounded against the ground in a rhythmic fashion, is an idiophone, as is a set of tap shoes. This class of instruments also includes bells, gongs, steel drums, xylophones, rattles, tambourines, cymbals, and even washboards. If it makes a sound when someone hits, shakes, scratches, or rubs it, it's an idiophone. If the instrument has a head made of animal skin or some other type of membrane, then it's a membranophone. Membranophones include drums, as well as one non-percussive instrument: the kazoo.

A steel drum is an example of an idiophone because when someone hits it, it vibrates and produces a sound. If its head were made of animal skin or some other type of membrane, it would be a membranophone. The vibrations from hitting the head of a membranophones are transmitted inside the container, causing the air to vibrate, and thus producing sound.

The best way to understand idiophones is to play one. In **Experiment 22:** *Creating an Idiophone*, you will turn some basic kitchen utensils into a world-class idiophone.

EXPERIMENT 22

Creating an Idiophone

Topic

How can a mixing bowl be turned into an idiophone?

Introduction

An idiophone is a musical instrument that produces a note when it vibrates. Idiophones can be shaken, rubbed, or hit. Idiophones have a long history; they date back tens of thousands of years. The earliest idiophones were probably nothing more than sticks, bones, and stones that were pounded or rubbed against each other. While there are slight differences in the way they are constructed, the principles that control how different idiophones produce sounds are basically the same. In this activity, you will construct an idiophone from a kitchen utensil and play it to see how you can control its volume and pitch.

Time Required

30 minutes

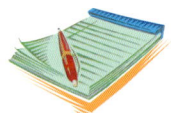

Materials

- large metal mixing bowl
- wooden spoon or drumstick
- several thick rubber bands
- chair

Safety Note No special safety precautions are needed for this activity. Please review and follow the safety guidelines before proceeding.

Procedure

1. Construct the beater for your idiophone. Wrap several large rubber bands around the handle of the wooden spoon or the end of the drumstick. Strike the mixing bowl with the rubber part. This will prevent damage to the bowl.
2. Place the bowl face up on a table. Gently strike the rim of the bowl and listen to the sound. Strike the bowl a little harder, and compare the sound to the first time you hit it.
3. Sit down in a chair with your legs spread slightly. Turn the mixing bowl upside down and hold it between your knees. (Hold it the way you would hold a bongo drum.) Use the beater to tap on the bottom of the mixing bowl. Compare the sound with the sounds in Step 2.

Figure 1

© Infobase Publishing

4. Take one of your thumbs and press hard against the bottom of the bowl. At the same time, use the beater to tap on the bottom of the bowl. Move your thumb to different locations on the bowl bottom while tapping, and listen to the sounds.

Analysis

1. What did the mixing bowl sound like when you first hit the rim with the beater? How did the sound change when you struck it harder?

2. What happened to the sound of the mixing bowl when you turned it upside down and struck the bottom with the beater?
3. What happened to the sound of the mixing bowl when you applied pressure to different places on the bottom of the bowl while striking it with the beater?

What's Going On?

Idiophones produce sound when they vibrate. Striking the mixing bowl on the rim with the beater transferred mechanical energy, which caused the bowl to vibrate. It sounded like a gong or church bell because the rim of the bowl was free to vibrate back and forth. Hitting the bowl harder caused a louder sound because you used more energy. This created sound waves with greater amplitude.

When you turned the bowl over and struck the bottom with the beater, the sound was different than when you hit the rim. It was softer and had a higher pitch. This is because the vibrating part of the bowl was much smaller. With most idiophones, smaller vibrating surfaces have faster vibrations, increasing the pitch of the note. When you pressed on the bottom of the bowl with your thumb and then struck it, the pitch changed even more. Pressing on the bowl bends the bottom of the bowl slightly, changing the shape of the vibrating surface. This effect is similar to how a steel drum works. A steel drum has a number of different-sized bends on its playing surface. Each one produces a different note when it is struck.

Our Findings
Analysis

1. Hitting the mixing bowl on the rim made it sound like a bell. Hitting it harder made the sound louder.
2. Hitting the bottom of the bowl produced a softer, higher pitched sound than hitting the rim.
3. Pressing on the bottom of the bowl while hitting it produced a variety of notes.

GONGS, TRIANGLES, AND BELLS

In the previous experiment, we saw how changing the surface of an object changes the sound it produces when hit. One of the big differences in the design of idiophones has to do with which vibrating surface produces the sound. In a steel drum or a wooden slit drum, one surface is made to vibrate, and it's the size and shape of that surface that controls the volume and pitch of the sound. For gongs, triangles, and bells, however, the sound comes from the vibration of the entire object. In **Experiment 23:** *Playing Resonant Water Glasses*, you will test to see how the mass of a vibrating object controls the pitch of the note and discover how a little bit of friction can go a long way toward making music.

Experiment 23: Playing Resonant Water Glasses

Topic

How does the mass of a vibrating object affect its pitch?

Introduction

Idiophones produce sounds by vibrating. In some cases, such as with a gong, the vibrations are set in motion when a musician strikes the instrument. In other cases, such as with a washboard or musical saw, sound is made by rubbing the instrument. One of the more ingenious idiophones using this approach was developed by Benjamin Franklin in the 1760s. Known as a glass armonica, the device was a series of glass bowls mounted on a rod. As the rod turned, the bowls spun. The musician played notes by rubbing his or her finger on the side of a bowl. In this activity, you will build a simplified version of Franklin's device and use it to test the relationship between the mass of a vibrating object and its pitch.

Time Required

30 minutes

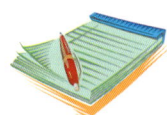

Materials

- 3 clean glass tumblers or wine glasses (must be glass), all the same size and shape, with thin sides
- 2 additional glass tumblers of different sizes than the ones above
- pitcher of water
- small bowl
- several paper towels

Safety Note No special safety precautions are needed for this activity. Use caution so that you do not break the glasses. Please review and follow the safety guidelines before proceeding.

Procedure

1. Place the three tumblers or wine glasses on the table in front of you. Leave the first glass empty. Fill the second about $1/3$ full of water. Fill the third about $2/3$ full.

2. Wash your hands with soap and water, and dry them on a clean paper towel. Fill the bowl with about an inch of water. Wet the tip of your pointer finger in the bowl. Rub the wet fingertip around the rim of the empty glass until it produces a sound. Wet your finger again and repeat the procedure with the glass that is $1/3$ full. Compare the sound of the two glasses. Repeat the procedure with the third glass.

Figure 1

© Infobase Publishing

3. Remove the two glasses with water in them. Put the two additional empty glasses next to the remaining glasses. Now order these three glasses in a row by size. Repeat the procedure in Step 2 and compare the sounds that they make.

Analysis

1. What happened to the water in the glasses when you began rubbing the rim? Why did you have to wet your finger first?

2. Which glass in Step 2 produced the highest note? Which produced the lowest note?

3. Which empty glass produced the lowest note? Which produced the highest note?

4. Based on your experiment, what is the relationship between the mass of an idiophone and its pitch?

What's Going On?

All objects vibrate at certain natural or resonant frequencies. Mass is one of the factors that controls the resonant frequency of an object. Heavy objects vibrate slower (lower frequency) than lighter objects. In this activity, it is not the air in the glass that is vibrating so much as the entire glass itself. Because the glass with the most water in it has the most mass, it will vibrate slower than the glasses with less water.

To make the glasses vibrate, you need to have just the right amount of friction between your finger and the rim of the glass. Wetting your finger will cause it to slide over the rim at first. As the water evaporates, the finger begins to drag more, producing friction. The sound is quiet at first, but then gets gradually louder as the rim of the glass begins to resonate more.

In theory, you can make almost any glass resonate. However, it is far easier to do with glasses that have thin sides. That's because a thinner piece of glass is more flexible than a thick piece, so it is takes less energy to get it vibrating.

Our Findings
Analysis

1. When you rub the glass, the water in the glass begins vibrating. The finger needs to be wet in order to control the amount of friction.
2. The glass that has the most water produces the lowest note, and the empty glass produces the highest note.
3. The largest glass produces the lowest note, and the smallest glass produces the highest note.
4. The greater the mass of a vibrating object, the lower the note it produces.

XYLOPHONES, GLOCKENSPIELS, AND REAL ROCK MUSIC

Over the years, the principle that a heavier mass will produce a lower note has been put to use in the construction of many different idiophones. In Unit 2, you experimented with different types of wood blocks to see how their physical condition affected the sounds they produced. One musical instrument that uses this concept is the xylophone. The word xylophone comes from the Greek words *xylon,* which means "wood," and *phone*, which means "sound." Put them together and you have the sound of wood!

If wood is not your favorite material, then you might want to check out a lithophone. This instrument has its musical bars made from stone (*lithos* is the Greek word for "stone"). Lithophones have never really caught on with rock bands, but they are popular in the Far East and Africa, where they are used in rituals and ceremonies.

If you are a fan of heavy metal, a metallophone may be your thing. These instruments have musical bars made from metal. Two of the more popular types are glockenspiels, which are portable instruments that are carried in marching bands, and chimes, which are used in orchestras and churches. In **Experiment 24:** *Testing Sounds of Metal Bracket Chimes*, you can try your hand at building your own metallophone made from some hardware.

A xylophone is part of the class of idiophones, which are instruments that make noise when someone hits, shakes, scratches, or rubs them. To play the xylophone, one hits the bars with a mallet.

EXPERIMENT 24: Testing Sounds of Metal Bracket Chimes

Topic

How does the size of a vibrating object control the pitch of an idiophone?

Introduction

An idiophone is a musical instrument that produces a note when it vibrates. Over the years, idiophones have been built out of many different materials including wood, metal, and even stone. In this activity, you will construct an idiophone made from steel angle brackets and test to see how the size of a bracket helps to control the pitch of a note.

Time Required

30 minutes

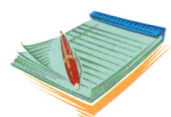

Materials

- 5 steel corner brackets in the following sizes: 4 in., 3 in., 2 ½ in., 2 in., and 1½ in. (10 cm, 8 cm, 6 cm, 5 cm, and 4 cm). These are available at most hardware or home improvement stores.
- screwdriver
- metal coat hanger (if it has paper on it, remove the paper)
- roll of cellophane tape
- roll of kite string or package string
- scissors

Safety Note No special safety precautions are needed for this activity. Please review and follow the safety guidelines before proceeding.

Procedure

1. Arrange the metal brackets on the table in front of you from smallest to largest. Cut five pieces of string, each about 12 in. (30 cm) long. Tie one string through the hole on the end of each bracket.
2. Hold the largest bracket in your hand. Tap it with the screwdriver and listen to the sound. Next, suspend the bracket by its string. Tap the bracket with the screwdriver, and compare the sound to the sound of the bracket when you held it in your hand.
3. Pick up the smallest bracket and hold it by its string. Tap it with the screwdriver and listen to the sound it makes. Compare this sound to the sound made by the largest bracket suspended by its string.
4. Arrange the brackets in order of increasing pitch and tie each one to the bottom of the coat hanger. Put a piece of tape around each string on the coat hanger so that the strings stay in place. It should look like Figure 1.

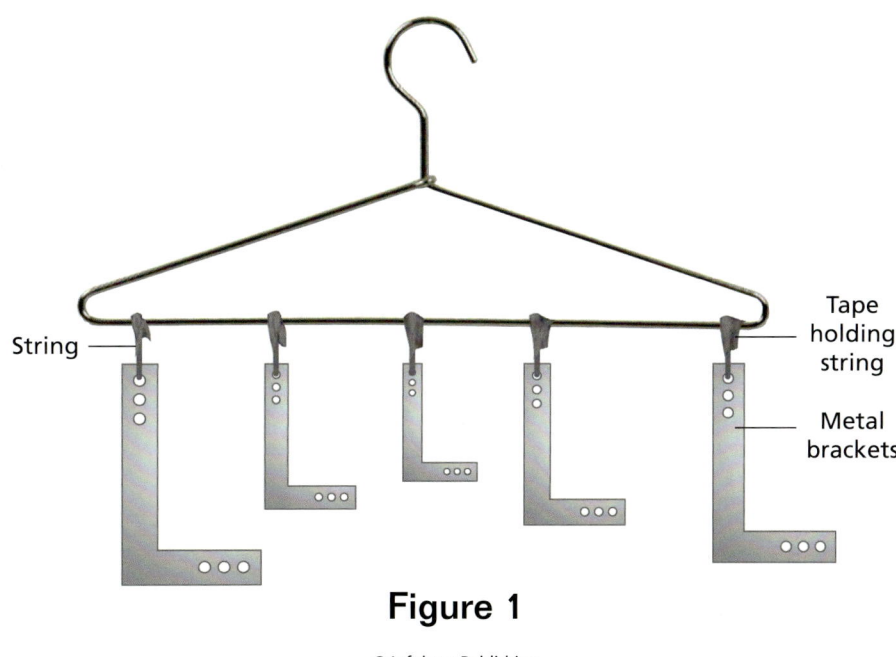

Figure 1

© Infobase Publishing

5. Hold the coat hanger in one hand by the hook, and use the screwdriver to strike each of the five brackets. Compare the sounds.

Analysis

1. How did the large bracket sound when you held it in your hand and hit it? How did this compare to the sound of the bracket when you held it by the string?

2. How did the sound of the large bracket compare to the sound of the smallest bracket?
3. What is the relationship between the size of the bracket and the pitch it makes?
4. Based on your experiment, why are triangles and gongs always supported by a string or cord?

What's Going On?

Idiophones produce sound when they vibrate. When you hit an angle bracket with the screwdriver, you used mechanical energy that was transferred to the bracket and made it vibrate. In order for the bracket to produce a note, however, it has to be free to vibrate. This is why you have to hang it from a string. It is also why gongs and triangles are almost always suspended by cords when they are played. If you were to hold these instruments in your hand, they would not work.

When you play a gong or a bell, you can control the volume of the instrument by controlling how hard you strike it. You cannot really control the pitch of the note. Because the entire object is vibrating, it produces one fundamental frequency. This is why bells and chimes often come in sets of varying size. The larger and more massive the bell is, the slower it vibrates, and the lower the pitch of the note that it produces.

Our Findings

Analysis

1. When the bracket is held in a person's hand, it makes a clacking sound. When the bracket is suspended by a string, it rings like a chime.
2. The large bracket produces a lower note than the smaller bracket.
3. The larger a bracket is, the lower is the note it produces.
4. Suspending a triangle from a string allows it to produce a note.

MEMBRANOPHONES: THE SKIN IS IN

No discussion of percussion instruments would be complete without information about membranophones. Membranophones include most drums. Instead of the entire instrument vibrating to produce a sound, the sound comes from a musician striking or rubbing some type of membrane or skin. Known as the head, this vibrating membrane usually covers a frame or container. When you play a membranophone, the vibrations from the head are transmitted to the air inside the container. This causes the air to vibrate, producing sound.

Like the other instruments that we have discussed so far, membranophones have a long history. They date back thousands of years. The bodies of early membranophones were usually made of wood or clay pots. These days, drum bodies are made out of wood, metal, and even plastic. Many people think of drums as being strictly rhythm instruments, but most can be tuned so that in the right hands, they can play a melody. In **Experiment 25:** *Controlling Drum Head Sound*, you will build several drums and use them to test how these percussive instruments get their pitch.

Experiment 25: Controlling Drum Head Sound

Topic
What factors control the pitch of a drum?

Introduction
Membranophones are instruments that have some type of vibrating membrane or "head." The most common type of membranophone is a drum. In early membranophones, the drum head was usually made out of animal skin. Modern drums often have plastic or other manmade coverings. Over the years, people have attached the head to the body of the instrument in several ways. They have used laces, pegs, nails, and glue.

Not all drums are membranophones. Steel drums and wooden slit drums are classified as idiophones, because neither has a head that vibrates separately from the rest of the instrument.

In this activity, you will test a few different membranophones to see how they can be used to produce sounds with different pitch.

Time Required
45 minutes

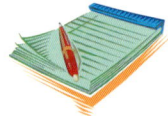

Materials
- large (2 lb or quart size), clean, empty plastic deli container with plastic lid
- small (1 lb or pint size), clean, empty plastic deli container with plastic lid
- small (13 oz – 16 oz), empty metal coffee can
- can opener
- ruler
- gallon-sized plastic storage bag
- scissors

- pencil
- 2 or 3 large, thick rubber bands
- person to assist you

Safety Note Use caution when removing the bottom of the coffee can. The edge of the lid will be extremely sharp! No other special safety precautions are needed for this activity. Please review and follow the safety guidelines before proceeding.

Procedure

1. Take the larger deli container and snap the lid on tight. Turn the container over and use the eraser end of the pencil to tap on the bottom of the container a few times. Now turn the container right side up and tap on the lip of the container a few times. Compare the sound that it makes when you tap on the lid to the sound that it made when you tapped on the bottom of the container.

2. Snap the lid onto the smaller deli container and place it next to the larger container. Use the eraser end of the pencil to tap on the lid of each container and compare the sounds that they make.

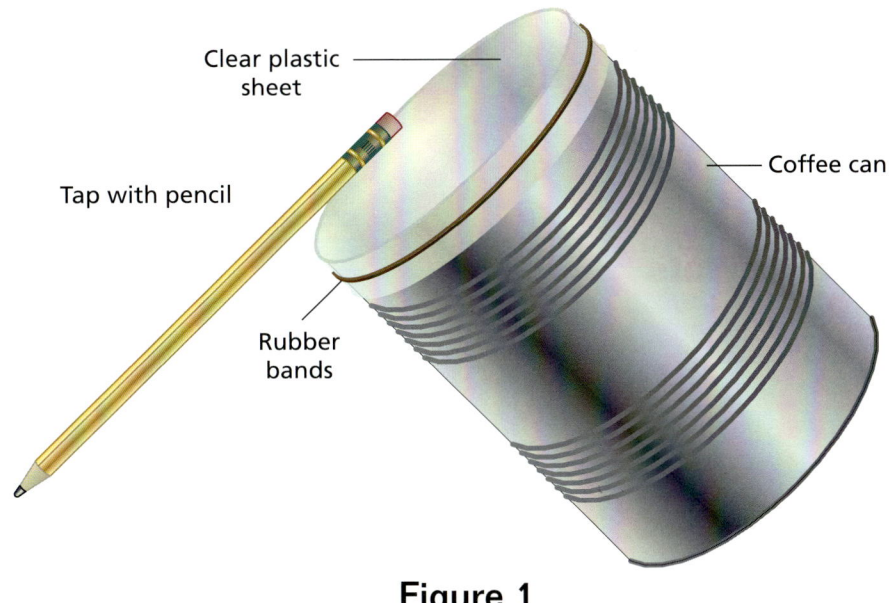

Figure 1

© Infobase Publishing

3. Use the can opener to remove the bottom lid of the metal coffee can so that you are left with a metal cylinder. The edge of the lid will be sharp. Cut one of the sides from one of the plastic bags. Trim the bag so that you have a sheet of plastic 8 in. x 8 in. (20 cm x 20 cm) in size. Stand the coffee can cylinder on one end on a table and place the plastic sheet over one opening. Put your hands around the rim of the cylinder and gently pull down on the plastic evenly on all sides so that it is stretched tight over the end of the coffee can. While you are pulling the plastic tight, ask your assistant to wrap two or three rubber bands around the rim of the can to hold the plastic sheet securely.

4. Hold the coffee can in one hand, and use the eraser end of the pencil to gently tap on the plastic sheet. As you continue tapping on the plastic sheet, gently squeeze and then release the sides of the can. Watch the plastic sheet as you squeeze the can and listen to the sound it makes. Compare this sound to the sound that came from the can when you did not squeeze the side.

Analysis

1. How did the sound coming from the large deli container change when you tapped on the bottom compared to when you tapped on the lid?
2. How did the sound of the large deli container compare to the sound of the small container?
3. What happened to the sound coming from the coffee can when you squeezed it while tapping on the plastic sheet?
4. What happened to the tightness of the plastic sheet when you squeezed the coffee can?

What's Going On?

Idiophones produce a sound when the entire instrument vibrates. In membranophones, the head of the instrument vibrates, causing the air inside to vibrate. In the first part of this experiment, the lid of the deli container was like the head of a drum. Though it is attached to the container, it is not part of the container, so it vibrates separately from the body of the container. Hitting the lid of the deli container produced a deeper, louder sound because it caused the air inside to vibrate. Hitting the container on the bottom produced a quieter sound because the container itself was vibrating the air around it.

The size of a drum helps control its pitch. The general rule is, the greater the volume of air in a drum, the lower the pitch, and the louder the sound it makes. This is one reason that a bass drum produces a much louder and deeper sound than a bongo drum. In this experiment, the sound from the smaller deli container was quieter and at a higher pitch than the larger container, because the larger container had a greater volume of air inside.

A second factor that controls the pitch of a drum is the tension, or tightness, of the head. Just like tightening a string on a guitar makes it play a higher note, tightening the head of a drum will increase the pitch. This is because a tighter drumhead will vibrate faster than one that is loose. Faster vibrations will produce sound waves with a higher frequency. When you squeezed the side of the coffee can, you reduced the tension of the plastic sheet on top. If you make the head of a large drum extremely tight, it can produce a higher pitch than a smaller drum.

Our Findings

Analysis

1. The sound that comes from tapping the bottom of the container is quieter and of a higher pitch than the sound that is made when the lid of the container is struck.
2. The sound from the larger container is deeper and louder than the sound from the smaller container.
3. The sound of the coffee can changes pitch when the sides are squeezed.
4. The tension of the plastic sheet changes when the sides of the coffee can are squeezed.

BIG BEATS: FROM TYMPANI TO TALKING DRUMS

Today, drums can be found in just about every country in the world. They come in a wide range of sizes and shapes, from tiny bongos to thundering tympani. Membranophones are often classified by body shape, but they also can be classified by the way they are played. Some drums are played using the hands, while others require sticks. Jazz musicians often will use metal brushes. Tympani players use padded beaters that resemble marshmallows on sticks. One of the more unusual types of drum is the *kalungu*, or "talking drum," commonly found in West Africa. These drums are played using a curved stick that is beaten and rubbed against the skin. The tones they produce are similar to the sounds used in the native language. In the hands of an experienced musician, the drums sound like they are talking.

Next, we'll take a look at some of the ways that modern technology has affected the science of music. From amplifying instruments to creating music with synthesizers and samplers, modern electronics has opened a new world for musicians and fans of music alike.

6

Modern Modes of Music

Let's examine the role that electricity and electronics have played in the development of modern music. Starting in the 1800s, scientists discovered the electron, the tiny particle in atoms that makes electricity possible. Scientists also discovered that electricity and magnetism were related; when electricity flowed, it created pulses of energy called electromagnetic waves. This text won't get into the details about how these waves work. Yet, these early breakthroughs allowed inventors to come up with a new way of amplifying and recording music.

SPEAK TO ME: A BRIEF HISTORY OF ELECTRONIC AMPLIFICATION

If you have ever attended a wedding or a rock concert, or even listened to a speech in an auditorium, you can appreciate the importance of electronic amplification. Before its invention, people making speeches or musicians playing to large audiences had to work hard to be heard. As we saw in Unit 1, designers of concert halls and theaters used their understanding of sound waves to maximize the projection of music. With acoustic instruments, however, even the best buildings had limits. One reason that classical orchestras and marching bands were so large was to make certain that the music would be heard. The more instruments playing at once, the louder the music would be.

Electronic amplification got its start in the late 1800s, but its origins had nothing to do with making music louder. In the early 1870s, Alexander Graham Bell, a Scottish immigrant living in the United States, was working on an idea for a "harmonic telegraph." At that time, most telegraphs could send only a single message at a time. They used Morse code and a device called a sounder, which would "click" out a message. A trained operator would then decode the message. Bell, who taught at a school for the deaf in Boston, came up with the idea of using a set of tuning forks instead of a sounder. By using different sound frequencies, Bell thought he could send several messages over the same line at the same time.

Bell teamed up with gifted engineer Thomas Watson. By June 1875, the two men had devised a system that used a set of vibrating metal reeds to create and transmit sound across telegraph wires. Each reed was attached to the coil of an electromagnet. When the reed vibrated, it made the coil of the magnet move. This generated an electric signal through the wire. One day, they were testing the system, and one of the reeds became stuck. As Watson worked to free it, Bell, who was in the other room, heard sounds coming across the receiver. It turned out that the reed was picking up and transmitting actual sounds. What they had built was an acoustic transmitter, or a very primitive microphone. This device would not only allow Bell to make the first practical telephone, but it would open the door for other uses, including sound amplification and recording.

After Bell received his patent for the new device, other inventors—including Thomas Edison—went to work to improve the efficiency of the Bell transmitter. Over the years, the transmitter evolved into the microphones we have today. Though modern microphones don't look anything like Bell's first acoustic transmitter, they work on the same principles.

A microphone is the first step in the process of electronic amplification. It picks up the sound and turns it into an electrical signal. In order to hear an amplified sound, you also need a device that takes an electrical signal and turns it back into a sound wave. This is what a loudspeaker does. A loudspeaker is a microphone turned backward. The first patent for a device similar to a loudspeaker was issued in 1877 to Ernst Siemens, a German engineer who had been experimenting with the affects of vibrations on electromagnetic coils even before Bell worked on his telephone.

These early speakers really served no practical purpose because, other than the telephone, there was no need to listen to sounds that were carried by electricity. Even so, inventors continued to work with the concept of converting electrical signals into sound. The first electric loudspeaker was a large horn that had a small moving diaphragm attached to its bottom end. When the diaphragm vibrated, it produced sound waves that

Lee de Forest's experiments with a vacuum tube (which he holds here circa 1910) led to the creation of the electronic amplifier.

were amplified by the horn—much the way the bell of a trumpet amplifies the sound of the musician's vibrating lips. As time went by, a number of important improvements were added to speaker design. These included a moving "voice coil" that produced a wider range of sound frequencies, and a vibrating paper cone to produce the sounds (rather than just having a small diaphragm inside a large horn).

The most important development happened when two General Electric engineers designed the first modern loudspeaker. In 1925, Chester Rice and Walter Kellogg outlined their idea for a compact, direct-radiating loudspeaker. This is basically the same type of speaker found in most audio equipment today. This new speaker design would be one of the key components in making musical instrument amplifiers a reality.

At the turn of the century, the big push for electronic amplification of sound didn't come from musicians. Instead, it came in the early 1900s with the development of radio. In the late 1800s, inventors such as Guglielmo Marconi and Nikola Tesla began using radio waves to send "wireless telegraph" messages through the air. These first radio signals used the same type of sounder as in traditional telegraphs. On Christmas Eve 1906, Canadian inventor Reginald Aubrey Fessenden used a technique called "amplitude modulation" (A.M., for short) to transmit the sound of a violin over the air. This was the first radio "broadcast," and it opened the door for a new industry.

Other inventors picked up on Fessenden's idea, but they faced a problem. The power of the early radio receivers was so small that people had to use tiny headphones to hear anything. This was not practical for groups of people that wanted to listen to the same radio broadcast. Then, in 1906, American inventor Lee de Forest began experimenting with a device called a vacuum tube. It had been invented in England a few years earlier. Through trial and error, de Forest discovered that if he modified the tube, it could be used to amplify the electronic signal from a radio. He called his new invention the audion, and the electronic amplifier was born.

Within a few short years, electronic amplifiers were being modified for use in radios and the newly developed record players. Finally, during World War I, people began using electronic amplifiers in the first public address systems. It wasn't until the mid-1920s that the thought of using electronic amplifiers for musical instruments really began to take shape. As it turns out, the instrument that pushed musical amplifiers into the spotlight was the guitar.

THE ELECTRIC GUITAR

One reason there was so little interest in electronic amplification at the turn of the twentieth century was because of the styles of music being played. Most of the music played in large concert halls was either classical music, performed by large symphony orchestras, or march music, performed by brass bands. There really was no need for amplification. In the early 1900s, however, artists such as Scott Joplin and Fats Waller had begun to introduce people to ragtime and jazz. This music began sweeping the nation, helped by innovations such as the record player and radio. At first, jazz was played mostly in clubs and small theaters, but as jazz musicians got more famous, they started playing in larger halls. Trumpet players, such as Louis Armstrong, still didn't need amplifiers because their instruments were quite loud. Guitar players, however, were facing a challenge.

Making a guitar loud enough to be heard had always been a problem. During the nineteenth century, steel strings and cross bracing improved the volume of the acoustic guitar. Guitar bodies also were made larger, giving them more air inside. One inventor, John Dopyera, went so far as to put a steel resonator on his wooden guitars.

Yet, in the 1920s, even the best acoustic guitars weren't loud enough to compete with brass and rhythm instruments in popular dance bands. This was especially clear when a band went into a studio to make records or play live radio broadcasts. In an effort to boost the sound level, some guitar players began putting microphones attached to amplifiers near or inside their guitars, but that led to technical problems. Not only would the microphones get in the way of their playing, but they would create an annoying sound called feedback. The only real solution was to somehow create a guitar that was directly amplified.

In 1924, an engineer named Lloyd Loar was working for the Gibson guitar company. He designed the first electric pickup for a guitar. A pickup was first designed for violas and string basses. It worked by "picking up" the vibrations of the instrument. Loar's pickup was crude and worked poorly because it was designed to work off the natural vibrations of the guitar.

The Frying Pan, held here by curator Ian Spero while promoting the 2007 Born to Rock exhibition in London, was the first ever electric guitar. Electric guitars pick up the vibration of the strings (instead of the vibration of the guitar) with an electromagnetic pickup, and amplify that vibration. The signal from the pickup is then sent to another amplifier, which enhances the sound.

In 1931, George Beauchamp—working with Adolph Rickenbacker at the Electro String Company—came up with a better idea. Instead of picking up the vibrations of the guitar, their device would pick up the vibrations of the strings. The pickup they used was electromagnetic. It consisted of a coil of wire wrapped around a bar magnet placed under the steel strings. A current was passed through the coil, creating a magnetic field that picked up and amplified the vibrations of the strings. The signal from the pickup was sent to another amplifier, which enhanced the sound.

In 1932, Beauchamp and Rickenbacker began marketing the first true electric guitar. Known as the Frying Pan, it was played on the musician's lap and was made of cast aluminum. This type of guitar was used primarily for Hawaiian music, which was popular at that time. This was not the type of instrument that a jazz, blues, or country-western guitar player would use. These players needed an electrified version of a more standard guitar, known as the Spanish guitar. Seeing the opportunity, several other manufacturers started building electrified guitars. The Gibson Company introduced the ES-150, one of the first truly successful electric guitars.

The first electrified Spanish guitars had a variety of problems. Because they were still hollow-bodied instruments that would resonate when they were played, feedback was a challenge. Many guitar players refused to touch these guitars, but some, such as jazz great Charlie Christian, showed how effective they could be. Hollow-bodied electric guitars were also popular among blues guitar players, such as T-Bone Walker and Muddy Waters, who actually used the feedback they created as part of their music.

Some guitar players started building their own guitars. One of these players was the legendary guitarist and inventor Les Paul. He decided to eliminate the guitar's hollow body. He reasoned that the guitar would still work, because the pickup worked off the vibrations of the strings, not the vibrations of the instrument. He mounted a guitar neck and pickup onto a solid 4-by-4 wooden post that looked like a small railroad tie. When he attached the strings to the bridge and picked some notes, the instrument not only played, but there was no feedback. Paul nicknamed his new guitar "the log" and while he never marketed it, he proved that solid-body guitars were the way to go. He would go on to design one of the most successful electric guitars of all time, the Gibson Les Paul, a favorite of many rock guitar players today.

Les Paul wasn't the only one experimenting with the idea of solid guitars. During the 1940s, Paul Bigsby and Leo Fender introduced similar guitars. In 1950, the Fender Guitar Company introduced the first mass-produced electric guitar, the Fender Telecaster. Then, in 1954, the company introduced its most popular guitar, the Fender Stratocaster. This guitar featured three pickups and a series of switches that would allow musicians to change the tone of the instrument. The Stratocaster, along with a series of compact amplifiers made especially for it, quickly became the favorite of a growing number of musicians who played a new type of music called rock and roll.

Les Paul invented a guitar with a solid body, which eliminated the feedback produced by hollow-bodied guitars. Paul is seen here in 1996.

By the early 1960s, rock musicians began testing the limits of what their electrified instruments could do. Guitar innovators, such as Jimi Hendrix and Eric Clapton, found that feedback could be a friend. Hendrix developed a technique to "play the feedback," getting all sorts of new sounds out of his guitar that still amaze and inspire guitar players today. His rendition of the American National Anthem at Woodstock in 1969 is one of the most incredible examples of what an electric guitar can do in the right hands.

Guitars and amps weren't the only electronic instruments to evolve in the 1960s. New types of electric pianos and organs also were being developed, along with devices such as wah-wah pedals, distortion boxes, and phase shifters. These devices were wired between the instruments and the amplifier to produce a greater range of sounds. In the 1960s, physicist Robert Moog invented possibly the biggest development of that decade. His compact synthesizers—called Moog synthesizers—not only changed the way music was played, but also changed the way music was made.

ELECTRONIC MUSIC: THE EARLY DAYS

Today, hearing a synthesizer as part of popular music is no big deal. Rock, country, hip-hop, and jazz musicians all use them. Classical music has even been written to feature synthesizers. Today, the average synthesizer is compact; it looks like a keyboard with many dials and knobs attached. It wasn't that long ago, however, that no one believed people could invent an electronic device to create music.

A synthesizer generates musical notes electronically, using almost none of the principles that control the way that wind, string, or percussive instruments work. The word *synthesize* means "to create something from a number of different parts." A musical synthesizer takes individual sound elements and puts them together to make musical notes. Robert Moog is probably the most famous name in synthesized music, but he wasn't the first person to come up with the idea of making music electronically. That honor goes Thaddeus Cahill, who was considering the idea back around the year 1900.

Thaddeus Cahill was a Washington, D.C., lawyer with an interest in music. He was so intrigued with the technological innovations of his day that he gave up law to become a full-time inventor. He spent his time working on minor improvements for pianos, and even invented a type of electric typewriter. He was most interested, however, in the idea of broadcasting music over telephone lines. At this time, telephone transmitters and receivers had so little power that the idea seemed impossible. Cahill had noticed that if a telephone was brought near an alternating current generator, it produced a sound on telephone lines. He also observed that generators turning at different speeds produced sounds of different pitches. He reasoned that if he hooked up a series of generators to telephone transmitters, he could use them to play music across telephone lines.

After spending several years on the project, he received a patent for a device he called the teleharmonium. In the patent application, he used the term "synthesize" when discussing the way his device made music. The first prototype was built in 1901. Though simple, it weighed almost 7 tons.

Cahill would go on to build other teleharmoniums, which he would later call dynamophones. Each was bigger than the one before. The final system, unveiled in 1906, cost more than $200,000. It contained more than 2,000 electrical switches in it, and weighed about 200 tons! Though Cahill's dynamophone worked well, its size and cost made it impractical. He did prove, however, that music could be made electronically. Eventually, his concept was scaled down and put to use by the Hammond Organ Company, one of the most successful producers of electronic organs in the world today.

By 1920, other pioneers of electronic music were at work, taking advantage of advances in amplifier and speaker design. One of the most innovative was Russian physicist Leon Theremin. Instead of using mechanical generators to make tones, Theremin used electronic radio tubes that **oscillated** at different frequencies. In later years, these types of devices would become

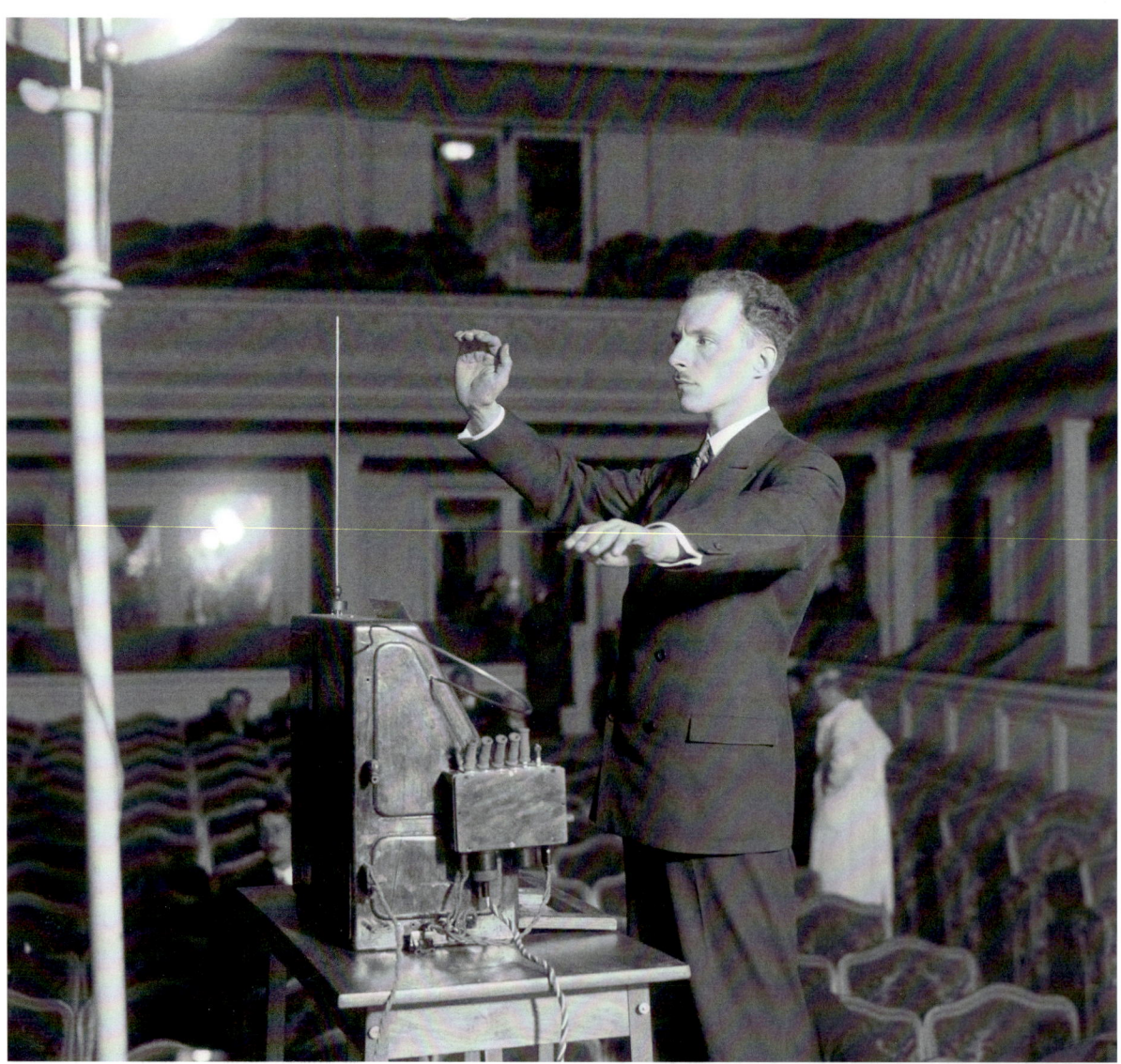

Leon Theremin's theremin, which he is shown playing (*above*) in 1927, involved moving one's hands near the device's metal rods, causing interference between radio waves and thus changing sounds.

known as oscillators and they would be a critical component of later synthesizers.

The instrument he invented was called by several different names, including a thereminvox and etherophone, but most people simply call it a theremin. The musician didn't have to touch a theremin to play it. Instead, it had two metal rods that acted similar to antennae. The rods sensed the positions of the musician's hands. Moving the hands caused interference between the radio waves, which changed the sounds. Like the teleharmonium before it, the theremin never really caught on, although some classical composers did write pieces for it. Probably the best known piece of music that uses a theremin is the Beach Boys song "Good Vibrations." The theremin plays the high, wavering tone in the background.

HOW MODERN SYNTHESIZERS WORK

By the end of World War II, advances in electronic circuits had led to many new technologies, including the first computers. In 1955, Harry Olson and Herbert Belar, working at the RCA labs in Princeton, New Jersey, unveiled the RCA Electronic Music Synthesizer. This was the first modern synthesizer that used oscillators, signal generators, and filters to create tones. Because it still used vacuum tubes, it was quite large; it took up most of a small room. It also couldn't be played directly. Instead, the instrument had to be programmed using paper tape. A second version, the Mark II, was placed at the Columbia-Princeton Electronic Music Center in 1959. That's where Robert Moog got into the act.

Moog had been interested in electronics and music from a young age. He built his own theremin in 1949 when he was just 15 years old, and would later go on to get his doctorate in engineering physics from Cornell University. Moog went to work at the Columbia-Princeton Electronic Music Center, where he saw the RCA synthesizer. He developed a number of electronic components that would make synthesizers compact and relatively inexpensive. In 1964, he demonstrated his first synthesizer that used a keyboard as the controller. Before this, synthesizers were usually controlled by rotary knobs and had to be programmed. By the early 1960s, transistors had replaced vacuum tubes in many electronic circuits. Moog incorporated these devices into his synthesizer, drastically reducing its size, weight, and cost. He had come up with a portable synthesizer that had a keyboard on the

Synthesizer pioneer Robert Moog holds a Moogerfooger synthesizer in 2000. Next to him is a 1971-era Minimoog synthesizer, which was one of the first portable, fairly affordable synthesizers.

outside and transistors on the inside, and could be played like a piano or organ.

At the heart of all modern synthesizers is the audio oscillator. This device changes a steady electric current to one that oscillates, or alternates, at a certain frequency. These oscillating currents then pass through filters, are amplified, and come out through speakers as sound waves. Through connections called patches, different oscillators can be combined to create new tones. Oscillators also can be manipulated to produce different wave forms with tone qualities. A sine wave, for example, produces a pure, clean note that sounds like a whistle. A square wave sounds like a mixture of an oboe and a flute. Sawtooth waves sound like a saxophone, and triangle waves sound like a flute.

Modern synthesizers also can incorporate special effects that can modify the music. Echo and reverb, which is short for *reverberate*, are standard effects which allow a musician make a note sound like it is being played in a large empty room. Other effects control the shape of the note's "envelope." The envelope describes the duration and volume of the note that is being played. A note can start out with a high volume and then get quieter, start out quiet and get louder, or stay the same volume for the entire time it is played. Many synthesizers also allow a musician to sample other sounds that have been prerecorded and stored in the instrument. A musician can add anything from bomb blasts to purring kittens into the music. Synthesizers also have sequencers, which can store sounds or musical notes as a rhythmic loop. One of the best examples of a sequenced synthesizer track can be heard in the opening of The Who's song "Won't Get Fooled Again."

THE FUTURE OF MUSIC

These days, it's hard to predict just where the science and art of music will take us. One of the most important developments in recent years has been integrating computers into synthesizers and recording equipment. A person can compose music on a laptop without having to know how to play a traditional acoustic instrument. In addition, hard drives can store music in digital formats, allowing composers to "sample" individual musical notes and phrases from existing pieces of music. Some musicians feel that this "cut and paste" approach isn't really musical composition, but it still takes a good ear and a creative person to make it work.

The truth is, from the earliest days, humans have composed music by sampling the sounds around them. Whether it was a bird chirping or a clap of thunder, people learned to mimic sounds with the instruments they developed. Digital sampling just makes this easier. In fact, over the past few decades, a growing number of composers have incorporated natural sounds into their music.

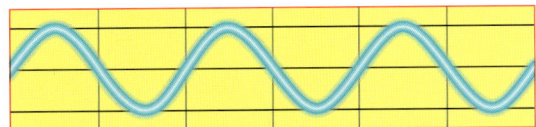
The sine wave is the pure frequency of the note, and it has a thin sound like a whistle

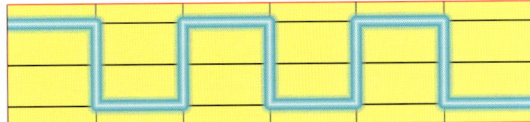
The square wave sounds like the mixture of an oboe and a flute

The triangle wave has a distinct flutelike sound

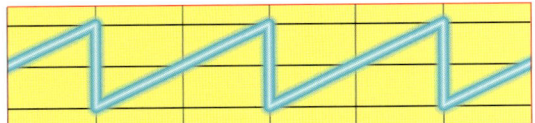
The sawtooth wave has a warmer and fuller sound, almost like a saxophone

© Infobase Publishing

Different sounds create different wave forms.

Each person views music a little differently. It's hard to define exactly what music is, but it's something that we all enjoy and, in many cases, need. Understanding the science behind music can make it sound that much sweeter!

Glossary

aerophone   an instrument such as a flute or trumpet that produces a sound when a column of air inside the instrument starts vibrating

amplitude   the maximum amount of displacement of a wave or a measure of how loud a sound is

chordophone   an instrument such as a guitar or violin that produces a sound with a vibrating string

compression   the part of a sound wave where the particles are squeezed together

crest   the highest point on a wave

forced vibration   the act of one vibrating object causing another object to vibrate—related to resonance

frequency   number of vibrations that happen per second in a wave; frequency controls the pitch of a sound or musical note.

fundamental   the main or primary frequency at which an object will vibrate

harmonics   the frequencies above the fundamental frequency at which an object will vibrate. Harmonics are higher pitch multiples of the fundamental.

hertz (Hz)   unit to measure frequency; one Hz is one vibration per second.

idiophone   a percussive instrument such as a bell or gong that produces a sound when the entire surface vibrates when struck or rubbed

longitudinal wave   a wave in which the particles vibrate in the same direction as the wave travels

membranophone   an instrument such as a drum that makes a sound when a membrane or skin is made to vibrate

oscillate   to alternate between two conditions or states

pitch   a measure of how high or low a musical note is

rarefaction   the part of a sound wave where the particles are spread apart

resonance   action when the vibrations from one object cause another object to vibrate at the same frequency

resonant frequency the natural frequency at which an object or instrument will vibrate

scale a gradual progression of notes that change in pitch from one to the next.

transverse wave a wave in which the particles vibrate at right angles to the direction the wave travels

trough the lowest point on a wave

vibrate to quickly move back and forth

wave a disturbance that repeats itself regularly in space over time

wavelength the distance between two identical points on two successive waves

Bibliography

Diagram Group. *Musical Instruments of the World.* New York: Sterling Publishing Co., 1997.

Editors of Consumers Guide. *How Things Work.* Lincolnwood, Illinois: Publications International Ltd., 1994.

Hewitt, Paul. *Conceptual Physics, 8th Edition.* New York: Addison Wesley, 1998.

Kaner, Etta. *Sound Science,* Reading, MA, Addison-Wesley, 1991.

Macaulay, David. *The Way Things Work.* Boston: Houghton Mifflin, 1988.

Rademacher, Johannes. *Music, An Illustrated Historical Overview.* Hauppauge, NY: Barrons Educational Services, 1996.

Robertson, William. *Stop Faking It! Sound.* Arlington, VA: NSTA Press, 2003.

Tomecek, Stephen M. *What a Great Idea!: Inventions that Changed the World.* New York: Scholastic, 2003.

Further Resources

Diagram Group. *Musical Instruments of the World.* New York: Sterling Publishing Co., 1997.

Hewitt, Paul. *Conceptual Physics, 8th Edition.* New York: Addison-Wesley, 1998.

Macaulay, David. *The Way Things Work.* Boston: Houghton Mifflin, 1988.

Richer, Margaret. *Teach Yourself Music Theory.* Chicago: McGraw-Hill, 2002.

Tomecek, Stephen M. *Electromagnetism and How It Works.* New York: Chelsea House, 2007.

Tomecek, Stephen M. *What a Great Idea!: Inventions that Changed the World.* New York: Scholastic, 2003.

Wade-Matthews, Max and Wendy Thompson. *Music: An Illustrated Encyclopedia of Musical Instruments and the Great Composers.* London: Lorenz Books, 2004.

Wood, Robert. *Sound Fundamentals.* Philadelphia: Chelsea House Publishers, 1999.

Web sites

Harmony and Proportion: Pythagoras: Music and Space
http://www.aboutscotland.com/harmony/prop.html
Learn how the Greek Philosopher Pythagoras first worked out the relationship between the length and tension of a vibrating string and the note that it plays.

How Electric Guitars Work
http://entertainment.howstuffworks.com/electric-guitar.htm
Discover the inner workings of the electric guitar and how it evolved over time.

Invention of the Electric Guitar
http://invention.smithsonian.org/centerpieces/electricguitar/invention.htm
Discover the complete history of the electric guitar. The site includes great links to some of the early innovators and performers.

Loudspeaker History
http://history.sandiego.edu/GEN/recording/loudspeaker.html
Discover the complete history of the loudspeaker and see how it has developed over the years.

Thaddeus Cahill's Teleharmonium
http://www.synthmuseum.com/magazine/0102jw.html
Get complete details and see the actual patent drawings of the first music synthesizer.

Picture Credits

Page

- 14: © Infobase Publishing
- 17: Kim Ruoff / Shutterstock
- 19: © Infobase Publishing
- 21: © Infobase Publishing
- 25: © Infobase Publishing
- 26: © Infobase Publishing
- 30: © Infobase Publishing
- 31: © Infobase Publishing
- 35: © Infobase Publishing
- 40: © Infobase Publishing
- 41: © Infobase Publishing
- 46: © Infobase Publishing
- 49: © Infobase Publishing
- 55: © Infobase Publishing
- 58: AFP Photo H.Jensen/ University of Tubingen/ HO Embargoed J/ Newscom
- 61: © Infobase Publishing
- 62: © Infobase Publishing
- 66: © Infobase Publishing
- 70: (*left*) James Steidl / Shutterstock
  (*right*) Milos Luzanin / Shutterstock
- 72: © Infobase Publishing
- 76: © Infobase Publishing
- 81: © Infobase Publishing
- 85: © Infobase Publishing
- 90: © Infobase Publishing
- 95: (*left*) Christopher Futcher / Shutterstock
  (*right*) Ben Smith/ Shutterstock
- 96: © Infobase Publishing
- 102: © Infobase Publishing
- 105: Newscom
- 106: © Infobase Publishing
- 111: © Infobase Publishing
- 112: © Infobase Publishing
- 116: © Infobase Publishing
- 121: Peter Albrektsen / Shutterstock
- 123: © Infobase Publishing
- 127: © Infobase Publishing
- 129: Anatoliy Samara / Shutterstock
- 131: © Infobase Publishing
- 135: © Infobase Publishing
- 141: Hulton Archive/Getty Images
- 144: Matt Dunham/AP Images
- 146: © Lynn Goldsmith/ Corbis
- 148: © Bettmann/CORBIS
- 150: Alan Marler/AP Images
- 151: © Infobase Publishing

Index

A

accordions, 94–95
acoustic engineers, 32
acoustic guitar, 143
Adam's apple, 50
aerophones. See wind instruments
amplifier, 88
amplitude and loudness. See also electronic amplification; volume, controlling instrument
   amplitude of wave, 19
   electricity and, 139
   energy and, 33
   pitch and, 43
   shape of wind instruments and, 109
   volume control and, 88
"amplitude modulation," 142
ancient music/instruments. See early music makers
animals and birds
   rhythm and, 64
   sounds, music and, 44, 151
archaeologists, wind instruments and, 59
Armstrong, Louis, 143
Australians, 106. See also didgeridoo

B

Beach Boys, 149
beat, rhythm and, 67
Beauchamp, George, 144
Belar, Herbert, 149
Bell, Alexander Graham, 140
bells, 120, 125, 132
Bigsby, Paul, 145

birds. See animals and birds
brackets. See metal bracket chimes, testing sounds of
brass instruments. See also trombone, creating sounds with
   brass construction of, 114, 117
   valves of, 100
   vibrating lips of musician and, 36
"broadcast," first radio, 142
bull-roarer, 119

C

Cahill, Thaddeus, 147–148
cello, 69. See also musical bows
chimes. See metal bracket chimes, testing sounds of
chordophones. See also stringed instruments
   aerophones and, 114
   idiophones and, 120
   musical bow as, 70
   pitch of strings and, 73
   resonators and, 89
   volume control and, 88
   zithers, 69–70
Christian, Charlie, 145
Clapton, Eric, 146
clarinet, 36, 95
compression/rarefaction, 26
concert halls/theatres, 29, 31–32
crest of wave, 19

D

de Forest, Lee, 141, 142
diaphragm, 51, 141–142

didgeridoo, 105, 108. See also resonance, making a didgeridoo
digital sampling, 151
Dopyera, John, 143
drum. See also membranophones
   resonance and, 86
   steel drum, 120, 124
   tympani, 138
   wooden slit drum, 125
drum head sound, controlling, 134–137. See also membranophones
   analysis/explanation, 136–137
   our findings/analysis, 137
   procedure, 135–136
   size, tension and, 137
   time required/materials, 134–135
   topic/introduction, 134
dynamophone, 147–148

E

early music makers
   animal sounds and, 44, 151
   bull-roarer, 119
   early instruments, 53
   idiophones, 122
   materials for instruments, 44
   membranophones, 133
   wind instruments, 58–59
echo and reverb, 151
Edison, Thomas, 140
electric guitar, 143–146
   electric pickup for, 143, 144
   first ever, 144
Electro String Company, 144

electronic amplification
 history of, 139–143
 microphone and, 88
electronic music: early days, 147–149
energy and wave motion, 17–18
 disturbance and, 18
 sound is energy, 12
etherophone, 149
experiment setup. See safety precautions

F

Fender, Leo, 145
Fender Guitar Company, 145
Fessenden, Reginald Aubrey, 142
"fifths," musical, 78
flutes. See also pitch, recorders/song flutes
 aerophones and, 94
 early instruments, 58–59
forced vibrations, 115
"fourths," musical, 78
Franklin, Benjamin, 126
frequency
 fundamental, the, 79
 measured in Hz, 20
 pitch and, 38, 82, 91, 137
 resonant frequency, 83
 wavelength and, 22, 98–99
Frying Pan, The, 144–145
fundamental, the, 79
future of music, 151–152

G

Gibson Company, 145
glass armonica, 126
glasses. See resonant water glasses, playing
glockenspiels, 129
gongs, 36, 86, 120, 125, 132
"Good Vibrations" (song), 149
Greek origin
 of 'idiophone,' 120
 of 'music,' 11
 of 'rhythm,' 67
 of 'xylophone,' 129
guitar. See also acoustic guitar; electric guitar; Spanish guitar
 in lute family, 69
 thickness of strings on, 80
 vibrating strings of, 36

H

Hammond Organ Company, 148
harmonicas, 94–95
harmonics, 93, 117
Hawaiian music, 145
Hendrix, Jimi, 146
hertz (Hz), 20
Hertz, Heinrich, 20
horn family. See also specific instrument
 as aerophones, 101, 108
 bell opening of, 110, 113, 142
 vibration of lips and, 95

I

idiophone. See also metal bracket chimes, testing sounds of
 chordophones and, 120
 Greek word origin, 120
 materials for instruments, 130
 membranophones and, 120–121, 136
 primitive, 53
 steel drum example of, 121
 xylophones, 129
idiophone, creating an, 122–124
 analysis/explanation, 123–124
 our findings/analysis, 124
 procedure, 123
 time required/materials, 122
 topic/introduction, 122
intervals. See octaves and intervals

J

jazz music, 143
Joplin, Scott, 143

K

kazoo, 120
Kellogg, Walter, 142

L

lab setup. See safety precautions
"language of science," mathematics as, 68
laptop, composing music on, 151
larynx, 49–50
lithophone, 129
Loar, Lloyd, 143
longitudinal waves, making
 analysis/explanation, 25–26
 described, 23
 our findings/analysis, 27
 procedure, 25
 time required/materials, 24
 topic/introduction, 24
 transverse waves and, 24
loudness and amplitude, 33. See also volume, controlling instrument
loudspeaker, 140–141
lute family, 69
lyre, 69, 70

M

Marconi, Guglielmo, 142
mathematical music, 68. See also Pythagoras
 scaling up, 79
 wind instruments and, 63
mathematics, 75
membranophones. See also drum head sound, controlling; drums
 attaching head of, 134
 idiophones and, 120–121, 136

Index **161**

skin or head of, 121, 133
tympani, 138
metal bracket chimes, testing sounds of, 130–132
    analysis/explanation, 132
    our findings/analysis, 132
    procedure, 131
    time required/materials, 130
    topic/introduction, 130
metal vs. wood, tone quality and, 114
Metallica, 69
metallopone, 129
microphone, 88, 140
Minimoog synthesizer, 150
Moog, Robert, 146, 147, 149–150
Moog synthesizers, 146
Moogerfooger synthesizer, 150
Mozart, Wolfgang Amadeus, 69, 88
Muses, ancient Greece, 11
music
    future of, 151–152
    Greek word origin, 11
musical bows
    evolution of, 71
    as simple chordophone, 70
    tension and, 73
musical saw, 126
musical scale, 79

N

natural frequency. See resonant frequency
note timing. See song rhythm vs. note timing

O

octaves and intervals, 75–78
    analysis/explanation, 77–78
    our findings/analysis, 78
    procedure, 76–77
    Pythagoras and, 75, 78
    time required/materials, 75–76
    topic/introduction, 75

Olson, Harry, 149
oscillation, wavelength and, 19
oscillators, 149, 150
overtones. See harmonics

P

Paleolithic Era
    bone flute and, 58
    written language and, 44
paleontologist, flute and, 59
panpipes, 60, 95
Paul, Les, 145, 146
percussive instruments. See drum head sound, controlling; volume, controlling instrument
physical properties, sound and, 13, 15–16
piano
    electric piano, 146
    soundboard inside, 91
    thickness of strings of, 80
    vibrating strings of, 36
piccolo, 36
pitch. See also string theory
    drum size and, 137
    frequency and, 38, 68
    string theory and, 74
    tension of string and, 82
pitch, mouth control of, 45–47
    analysis/explanation, 47
    data table, 46–47
    our findings/analysis, 47
    procedure, 45–46
    singing a song and, 48
    time required/materials, 45
    topic/introduction, 45
    vibration of mouth/lips, 47
pitch, recorders/song flutes, 96–99
    air column and, 98–99
    analysis/explanation, 98–99
    mouthpiece and, 96–97, 98–99
    procedure, 97–98
    time required/materials, 97
    topic/introduction, 96–97

pitch, speed of vibrations and, 39–42
    analysis/explanation, 41–42
    our findings/analysis, 42
    procedure, 40–41
    time required/materials, 39
    topic/introduction, 39
pitch, thickness of strings and
    analysis/explanation, 82
    our findings/analysis, 82
    procedure, 81
    Pythagoras and, 79, 82
    time required/materials, 80
    topic/introduction, 80
pitch, tube length and, 60–63
    analysis/explanation, 62–63
    our findings/analysis, 63
    procedure, 61–62
    time required/materials, 60
    topic/introduction, 60
pitch pipe, 101
Pythagoras
    mathematics and, 75
    octaves, fifths and, 77–78
    string theory of, 74
    tension of string and, 82
    thickness of strings and, 79, 82

Q

quality of sound, 93

R

radio "broadcast," first, 142
ragtime music, 143
rarefaction/compression, 26
RCA Electronic Music Synthesizer, 149
recorders. See also pitch, recorders/song flutes
    materials for instruments, 117
    mouthpiece of, 96–97
recording equipment, 151
reed family. See under wind instruments

reflecting sound waves
   analysis/explanation, 31–32
   concert halls/theatres and, 29, 31–32
   described, 28
   our findings/analysis, 32
   procedure, 30–31
   time required/materials, 29
   topic/introduction, 29
reflection, waves and, 28
resonance
   described, 83, 84
   in wind instruments, 105
resonance, making a didgeridoo, 106–108
   analysis/explanation, 107–108
   our findings/analysis, 108
   procedure, 107
   time required/materials, 106–107
   topic/introduction, 106
resonance, musical instruments and, 84–87
   analysis/explanation, 86
   our findings/analysis, 87
   procedure, 85–86
   time required/materials, 84
   topic/introduction, 84
resonant frequency
   of buildings and bridges, 86
   didgeridoo and, 105
   mass and, 128
   objects vibrating at, 88, 117
   stringed instruments and, 83
resonant water glasses, playing, 126–128
   analysis/explanation, 127–128
   our findings/analysis, 128
   procedure, 127
   time required/materials, 126
   topic/introduction, 126

resonators, amplification and, 89–92
   analysis/explanation, 91–92
   our findings/analysis, 92
   procedure, 90–91
   soundboard and, 91
   time required/materials, 89
   topic/introduction, 89
resonators, chordophones and, 89
reverb and echo, 151
rhythm. See also song rhythm vs. note timing
   Greek word origin, 67
   rocking in, 64
   timing of notes and, 68
   two parts of, 67
Rice, Chester, 142
Rickenbacker, Adolph, 144
rubber bands. See pitch, thickness of strings and

S

safety precautions, 8–10
   chemicals and, 9
   equipment and, 9
   finishing up, 10
   general precautions, 8
   heating substances, 9–10
   preparation for experiments, 8
   protecting yourself, 9
   reviewing experiment, 8
sawtooth waves, 150–151
scales, musical, 79
science of sound, 11–12
shape, wind instruments and, 110–113
   analysis/explanation, 112–113
   bell opening and, 110, 113
   cylinder/ear bud and, 112–113
   our findings/analysis, 113
   procedure, 111–112
   time required/materials, 110
   topic/introduction, 110

Siemens, Ernst, 140
sine wave, 150
slide valves, 100, 103
slide whistle, 103
song rhythm vs. note timing, 65–67
   analysis/explanation, 67
   our findings/analysis, 67
   procedure, 65–66
   topic/introduction, 65
sound as energy, 12
"sound board," 91
sound makers, selected, 13–16
   analysis/explanation, 15–16
   data table, 15
   our findings/analysis, 16
   physical properties and, 13, 15–16
   procedure, 14
   time required/materials, 13
   topic/introduction, 13
sound waves. See also waves
   amplitude, loudness and, 33
   compression/rarefaction, 26
   nature of, 23
   oscillators and, 150–151
   pitch, frequency and, 38–42
Spanish guitar, 145
square wave, 150
steel drum, 120, 121, 124, 125
Stone Age. See Paleolithic Era
Stratocaster guitar, 145
string theory. See under Pythagoras
stringed instruments, 69–70. See also chordophones; specific instrument
   bridge on, 91–92
   chordophones, 69–70
   lute family, 69
   tone quality of, 93
   wooden construction of, 114
Sydney, Australia, opera house, 32

synthesizers
  as commonplace, 147
  early synthesizers, 146
  future of music and, 151
  modern, 149–151
  sequencers for, 151

T
Tacoma Narrows Bridge, 86
"talking drum," 138
telegraphs, 140, 142
teleharmonium, 147, 149
tempo, rhythm and, 67
Tesla, Nikola, 142
Theremin, Leon, 148
thereminvox, 149
thickness of strings, pitch and, 79
timbre, 93
transverse waves, 23, 24
tree falling in forest question, 13
triangles, 125, 132
trombone, creating sounds with, 101–104
  analysis/explanation, 103
  our findings/analysis, 103–104
  procedure, 102–103
  slide of instrument, 103
  time required/materials, 101
  topic/introduction, 101
trough of wave, 19
trumpet, 101, 142
tuba, 36, 39, 101
tube length. See pitch, tube length and
tuning fork, 26
Turk, Ian, 59
tympani, 138

V
vacuum tube, 141
valves, 100
vibrating rubber bands. See pitch, thickness of strings and

vibrating string, tension on, 71–74. See also frequency
  analysis/explanation, 73
  our findings/analysis, 73–74
  procedure, 72–73
  time required/materials, 71
  topic/introduction, 71
vibrations through different materials, 115–118
  analysis/explanation, 117
  forced vibrations and, 115
  our findings/analysis, 118
  procedure, 116–117
  time required/materials, 115–116
  topic/introduction, 115
violin. See also musical bows
  amplification and, 109
  in lute family, 69
  resonance and, 86
  "stop" for string, 79
  timbre of, value and, 93
vocal cords, controlling, 49–52
  analysis/explanation, 51
  diaphragm and, 51
  our findings/analysis, 51–52
  procedure, 50–51
  singing a song and, 48
  time required/materials, 50
  topic/introduction, 49–50
  voice box and, 49–50
voice box, 49–50
volume. See amplitude and loudness; resonators, amplification and
volume, controlling instrument, 34–37
  analysis/explanation, 36–37
  our findings/analysis, 37
  procedure, 35–36
  time required/materials, 34
  topic/introduction, 34

W
Walker, T-Bone, 145
Waller, Fats, 143
washboard, 120, 126
water glasses. See resonant water glasses, playing
Waters, Muddy, 145
Watson, Thomas, 140
"wave cheer," 18
wave motion and energy, 17–18
wavelength
  frequency and, 22, 98–99
  measurement of, 19
waves. See also sound waves
  disturbance and, 18
  parts of, 19
  reflection and, 28–32
  simple wave, 19
  water and, 17, 28
waves, vibration speed and size affect upon, 19–22
  analysis/explanation, 22
  data table, 21
  our findings/analysis, 22
  procedure, 20–21
  time required/materials, 20
  topic/introduction, 19–20
"whistle flute," 96
whistling. See pitch, mouth control of
Who, The, 151
wind instruments. See also horn family; shape, wind instruments and; specific instrument
  air column and, 98–99
  bell of, 110
  didgeridoos, 105, 108
  early instruments, 58–59
  reed family of, 94–95
  resonance and, 86, 105
  volume control and, 36
  wood vs. metal, 114
windpipe, 49, 51
"Won't Get Fooled Again" (song), 151

wood blocks, musical, 54–57
    analysis/explanation, 56–57
    condition of wood and, 54, 57
    data table, 56
    our findings/analysis, 57
    procedure, 55–56
    time required/materials, 54–55
    topic/introduction, 54
wood vs. metal, tone quality and, 114
wooden slit drum, 125
Woodstock, 146
woodwinds. See also specific instrument; wind instruments
    materials for instruments, 114, 117
    pitch control of, 100
    vibrating reeds of, 36

X

xylophone
    Greek word origin, 129
    as idiophone, 120

Z

zithers, 69–70

About the Author

STEPHEN M. TOMECEK is a scientist and part-time jazz drummer who also plays the bass and saxophone. He is the author of over 30 nonfiction books for both children and teachers, including *Bouncing & Bending Light,* the 1996 winner of the American Institute of Physics Science Writing Award. Steve also works as a consultant and writer for The National Geographic Society and Scholastic Inc.